Let the children come to me.
Don't stop them.
For the Kingdom of God belongs to those
who are like these children.

Then He took the children in His arms,
placed His hands on them and blessed them.
(Mark 10:14, 16 NLT)

Helping Hurting Children:

A Journey of Healing

*A Workbook Designed for Children
to Learn How to Cope with Losses in their Lives*

Martha Faircloth Bush

WestBow
PRESS
A DIVISION OF THOMAS NELSON

WestBow Press books may be ordered through booksellers or by contacting:

WestBow Press
A Division of Thomas Nelson
1663 Liberty Drive
Bloomington, IN 47403
www.westbowpress.com
1-(866) 928-1240

ISBN: 978-1-4497-8527-7 (sc)

Library of Congress Control Number: 2013903292

Printed in the United States of America

WestBow Press rev. date: 03/07/13

Table of Contents

Special Message to Caring Adult

Dear Caring Adult:

As you thumb through the pages of this workbook perhaps you will think of a child or a group you would like to take on this journey.

If so, I would encourage you to <u>acquire the accompanying Reference Guide</u> that goes along with the workbook. The purpose of the Reference Guide is to help you, the caring adult, meet some of the challenges you might face as you travel this journey with a child.

It is written with the intent to enlighten you to a child's emotional state of mind during a time of loss in his life. Prayerfully, it will keep you from being "caught completely unaware," as you help him process his grief and answer the many questions he might have as a result of his loss. I encourage you to read through it prior to beginning the journey and refer to it often so that you can better understand and support him.

*As the author of this guide, it is my prayer that by **<u>Helping Hurting Children</u>**, you, too, may experience a healing in your own life. May God bless you and the children as you embark on a **<u>Journey of Healing.</u>***

Martha Bush

DEDICATION

This guide is dedicated to the memory of Melba Berkheimer and Dustin Brack.

Melba

The late Melba Berkheimer was my mentor and friend at Community Church in Orange, Texas, where she and her husband, David, were pastors for over thirty years. Melba's teaching on *The Grieving Process* helped many people discover healing after facing losses in life. She spent many years studying and researching this subject and passing on her knowledge to others. Her legacy lives on in the many lives she touched, myself included. Now, her work will continue as it touches the lives of children with principles from her teachings included in this guide. Without Melba's influence on my life, this book would not be a reality.

Dustin

Dustin's life was cut short at the young age of 11 in an accident, but not before he had made an impact on many people's lives. When Dustin met someone, his main objective was to find out if that person had a relationship with Jesus. He asked his music teacher before his first lesson if she knew Jesus. When she told him that she did know Jesus, he replied, "Okay, now we can begin."

The struggles Dustin's family had in coping with his death while still continuing to serve as children's church pastor at their local church, is briefly described on page four in the endorsement written by his parents, Dan and Darla Brack.

ACKNOWLEDGEMENTS

Many thanks to...

My daughter, Heather, whose idea it was for me to venture into my first writing project. Her prodding, prompting, and encouraging words led me into one of the most exciting and fulfilling adventures of my life.

My husband, Glen, who worked many hours assisting me with his computer and document knowledge throughout the process of writing this book; I could not have done it without him.

My illustrator, Mel LeCompte, Jr. for his illustrations that I'm sure will capture the heart of every child reading this book. Mel has received two first place awards for his cartoon illustrations from the Louisiana Press Association. He is also the author and illustrator of two children's books: *The Ice Cream Cow*, and *T-Boy and the Terrible Turtle*.

Dr. Dianne Haneke, author and retired professor, who edited the first draft and who taught me much about my first plunge into writing from her years of teaching and writing.

My friends in Gloria Lee's Bible Study Group, Orange, Texas who edited the second draft.

My daughter, Crystal, and sons-in-law, Tim and Hoit, who encouraged and cheered me along on my first writing adventure.

My mother, Faye, who prayed for children's lives to be touched through this book.

All the professionals at Westbow Press who helped guide me through the publishing process of the workbook and reference guide.

And most of all I want to acknowledge and thank Jesus for healing this "little girl's broken heart" and giving me the desire to pass His message of healing onto other children.

ENDORSEMENTS

We lost our son, Dustin, at the age of 11 in an accident. Our two daughters, Lindsay and Haley, were left trying to make sense of a shattered home where life would never be the same. They experienced times at school, church, and with friends where they were just not understood and many times felt their pain went unheard.

This book is a life-saver for parents, grandparents, children's pastors, and teachers to have some understanding of how to help a child who has experienced loss. I believe this will be a valuable tool that will aid in the healing of many children who wake up one day and find their lives turned upside down by the loss of a loved one.

If you want to truly minister to the children who are hurting with grief, then you will definitely want to keep this workbook at your fingertips. As parents who have walked this path, this book is like bread and water to us as we try to help our children.

Reverend Dan and Mrs. Darla Brack

Children's Church Pastors, Community Church
Orange, Texas

Children suffer various losses during their childhood with little or no knowledge of how to cope with those losses. As children grieve differently than adults, the normal grieving responses may not be recognized; consequently, children are often left to deal with their grief alone. I am pleased to recommend this resource as an easy-to-use guide for those parents, grandparents, children's church leaders, or others who desire to help, but who may have felt powerless or unsure as to how to do so.

Virginia G. Johnson, Licensed Professional Counselor

Credentials: LBSW, LCDC, M.Ed. LPC

Martha has done an excellent job taking the most common steps in dealing with a loss and putting them in a very teachable format for children. As I read the manual, I knew it would be a great tool for anyone working with children. As a children's pastor for several decades, I plan on applying these principles to help children work through losses in their lives. Whether you are a parent, a teacher, a mentor, or a counselor, you will truly be blessed by knowing and sharing these principles.

Rev. Lisa Ellermann

Founder of:
  Camp His Way Children Camp, Jasper, Texas
  Camp His Way Children Camp, Chennai, India

FOREWORD

I have known Martha Bush as her pastor for well over two decades. During that time she has studied, taught, and helped both adults and children to find their identity in Christ. She is writing from experience, deep study and much success in helping people to overcome past hurts, losses, abuses and rejections.

She knows the valuable treasure that lies in the hearts of God's kids and seeks to release it. So many see the future as hopeless and themselves as worthless due to ill treatment and circumstances. Their whole interpretation of life is skewed so that everything they do fails before they get started, thinking that they are worthless without value to both God and man.

Can abused and hurting children be reached with this message? If they are capable of learning several languages at the same time before the age of six as well as thinking in those languages, surely God's loving Word and the compassion of living human beings can reach them deep inside. Besides knowledge, Martha knows that the presence and love of God can easily be experienced and felt in their lives.

I know Martha Bush. I've seen her efforts, work of love, and successes. I know the principles and the God she serves works miracles in the lives of adults and children. So, I wholeheartedly recommend her writings.

David Berkheimer

Former pastor of Community Church (32 plus-years)
Orange, Texas

Chapter 1

Beginning the Journey

Did you ever receive a blue ribbon for winning something special? Perhaps you might have won a relay race, the spelling bee, had perfect attendance in school, or read the most books in the summer reading program. It feels good to win, doesn't it? I believe we can safely say that, "Nobody likes to lose; we all want to be winners!"

As much as we all like to win, unfortunately, **losing is a normal part of life,** even in the lives of children like you. Anytime you lose something or someone very special to you, it is going to hurt and cause sadness in your life. However,

THE GOOD NEWS IS:

You <u>can</u> continue to be happy after a loss in your life.

To find happiness in life after a loss, this book will take you on a ***Journey of Healing***. As with any journey you take, there will be interesting things for you to see and learn along the way. Oh yes. There will also be a time set aside just for fun.

So, let's start at the beginning of the journey and see what is in store for you.

Beginning the Journey

Your journey starts now, and from this point on, you will be making stops along the way. At each of these stops, you will learn something that will help you recover from any loss you have experienced.

For example:

- On your first stop, you will learn what the word **Loss** means and the different types of losses.

- Next, you will learn what the Bible says to do about those losses as you explore the meaning of the word **Grieve.**

- As you continue on your journey, you will be given an opportunity to experience some of the steps that are commonly used to grieve a loss. Those steps are:

  1. **Recognizing Feelings**
  2. **Expressing Feelings**
  3. **Forgiving Others**
  4. **Asking Others to Forgive You**
  5. **Accepting Losses**

What to Pack

Just like any trip you take, you must pack a few things to bring with you. For this trip, you will need to pack the following items.

❖ **Your Bible:** At every stop, not only will you learn something very important about each of the five steps mentioned above, but you will also read a Bible story that relates to each of those steps. You will learn more about the lives of such familiar Bible characters as: Joseph, David, Cain, Abel and many more. As you read the Bible story, scriptures will be pointed out for you to memorize. These memory verses will stay with you for your entire life.

❖ **Crayons, markers, and pens:** At every stop, you will also be given an opportunity to share your memories of the loss you have experienced, using the activities that have been provided for you. As you share your memories, you may choose to draw, paint, write or do whatever works best for you to express yourself. This will be your own special place where you can go and be yourself without fear or embarrassment.

Meet Some New Friends

Five other kids will be traveling with you on your **_Journey of Healing._** They will be sharing their stories about losses they have experienced in their lives. Their pictures are shown throughout the book in cartoons, but their stories are true.

Let's meet those kids now.

Hadley   Crystal   Heather   Hannah   Zach

Bubby the Rabbit

Bubby the Rabbit will also be traveling along on this journey with you. Bubby will be giving you scriptures and tips to help you build up your self-esteem. Self-esteem means how you feel about yourself, the opinion you have of yourself, and how much value you place on yourself.[1] Bubby will help you see yourself as God sees you. This will give you the confidence to become all that God has created you to be. Bubby will also be hopping in at other places along the journey, so watch for him.

A special caring adult will be traveling with you, too. This adult might be your parents, grandparents, children's minister at church, school counselor, or your foster parent. These adults will be traveling with you to listen as you pour out your heart about a loss you have experienced. They will be close by your side to comfort and pray with you along your **_Journey of Healing._**

Keep two things in mind throughout your journey:

(1) Always Ask Any Question That Comes to Your Mind

Sometimes children are afraid to ask a question because they think it might sound "dumb." The fact is, there are no dumb questions. We all learn by asking questions. So always ask anything that comes to your mind that you'd like someone to answer for you.

(2) It's O.K. to Play During Sad Times

Sometimes children feel that it is wrong to play and have fun during a sad time in their life. It is not wrong to play during times of sadness. So, keep playing and having fun with your friends.

Are you ready to begin your journey?

Believe for good things to happen!

 **First stop:** Learning what the word **Loss** means.

My Journey of Healing Begins

Paste your picture here

Date: _____

Chapter 2

What Does Loss Mean?

When Heather was in the first grade, she went to school one day all excited. It was the day she was to audition for the lead singing role in her school's Christmas play. Her heart's desire was to perform on the big stage in the school auditorium. Sadly, Heather lost the audition.

When she came home from school that day, she crawled up on her mom's lap and began sobbing her little heart out. "Mrs. Hall picked Trina instead of me. I don't even want to go to the Christmas play now. I can't stand to see Trina singing all those songs that I wanted to sing. It hurts soooooo bad, Mom!"

At six years of age, Heather had just experienced her first loss in life.

What exactly does the word **loss** mean?

> *A loss is a separation from someone or something of special value to you.*

Sometimes without even realizing it, different types of losses are being tossed all around us like juggling pins wherever we go. Take a closer look at a few of the different types of losses.

Examples of Losses

(1) not making the football team or simply not getting to play

(2) not having a dress to wear for a special occasion

(3) a friend saying: "I don't want to play with you anymore."

(4) being sick or the illness of a loved one

(5) having anything stolen from you, such as your skates or bicycle

(6) your sister or brother graduating from high school and leaving home

(7) having someone you love in jail

(8) failing a test in school or not passing to the next grade

(9) a family member or friend being addicted to drugs or alcohol

(10) abuse: being hit real hard, called bad names, touched inappropriately

(11) school violence: fights, gangs, weapons

(12) natural disasters: tornadoes, hurricanes, storms, floods, earthquakes

Are you thinking - - - "I thought a loss was something like when my Grandpa died?" As devastating as it is to lose your Grandpa, losses also occur in many other areas of children's lives.

Anytime you have been separated from
someone or something
of special value to you, a loss has occurred.

Let's ask our Journey Friends traveling with us to tell us about the loss they have experienced.

Experiences of our Journey Friends

Hadley

It was 10'oclock at night and my dad was rushed to the hospital very sick. The doctor examined him and told us that he had had a massive heart attack. Throughout the night, my aunts, uncles, and cousins began arriving at the hospital. They would go into the room to see Daddy and come out crying.

As I sat all alone out in the hallway, I wondered, "Why is everyone crying; Daddy is going to be alright."

All of a sudden, I heard a loud groan coming from Daddy's room. I raced into the room and saw him grab his chest. Immediately, the nurses rushed my mother and me out of the room, into the elevator, and sat us down in the waiting room downstairs.

About thirty minutes later, I looked toward the stairs and I saw two nurses and a doctor coming toward us. I thought, "They are coming to tell us Daddy is okay and we can take him home."

The doctor knelt down beside my Mother and me, and said: "I'm sorry to tell you this, but Roy has died." I had to get out of that hospital, so I took off running and screaming with my cousin chasing after me.

I lost a very special person in my life -- my dad.

Crystal

Jay was a "bully" and he picked me to be his main target. We lived in the same neighborhood, and he was one of the kids I played with after school every day.

His bullying started with him punching me in the face. After taking a few of his punches in the face, I finally told my mom and she talked to Jay's mom. His mom said, "Oh, he's just playing; boys will be boys." So, Jay kept it up until my mom and dad said I could no longer play with the other kids in the neighborhood when Jay was around.

But, that didn't stop Jay. He found me at school, and kept on punching me and pulling my hair. What embarrassed me so much was when he started making fun of the way I looked in front of the other kids. When I cried, he'd laugh at me and call me a "cry-baby."

He told me that I'd better do everything he said, or he would really hurt me. He also threatened to hurt my little sister if I told the teacher what he was doing to me. I lived in fear, and I dreaded going to school every day.

I started having a low opinion of myself and felt I had no value. I even started to believe that I was ugly, just like Jay had said.

I lost my self-esteem.

Heather

For two weeks, my sister and I had heard Mom and Dad talking about moving to another state. "Surely, they can't mean that," we thought. But, the night finally came when they made the grand announcement that we definitely would be moving because of my dad's job.

I was 11 years old and my sister was 15 at the time of the move. I had lived on Deerlick Lane in New Orleans in the same house since I was 2 years old. My best friend, Stacy, lived next door to me. New Orleans was also where I had always gone to church and school.

One month after Mom and Dad told us we were moving, a big moving van pulled up in our yard. Two men came into my room, started packing all my things into big boxes, and carrying them out to the moving van. I wanted to grab one of the big boxes and hide in it forever.

That day, **I lost my friends, school, church, and my house that I loved so much.**

Hannah

I had a pet dog, name Fala. He came to live with me when I was six years old. One day I came home from school, got my snack, and turned the TV to my favorite after-school show. Just as I was getting settled down, my mom told me that she wanted to talk to me. It was then she told me Fala had gotten real sick while I was at school. Mom said she had rushed him to the vet, but he died in the vet's office.

"Where is he, where is he?" I asked. Mom explained that the vet had put Fala in a card board box, and she had placed him on Dad's workbench in the garage. She told me that Dad would bury him in our backyard when he got home from work so that Fala would always be near us.

I rushed to the garage; I had to see Fala one more time. I took him from the box, cuddled him in my arms, and walked around in the garage with him a long time. My heart was broken.

I finally put him back in the box and went back into the living room with my mom. I lay my head down in her lap and cried and cried, while I held Fala's collar tightly in my hand.

I lost a very special friend. Fala, my play friend and pet dog, died.

Zach

One night I was in my room doing my homework. All of a sudden, I heard Dad call for my little brother and me to come into the living room. "Your mom and I have something to talk to you guys about," he said.

I thought we were in trouble for doing something wrong, and they were going to punish us. But, what came out of their mouths took me by surprise.

Mom and Dad explained they had problems they could not solve, and were not happy with each other. So, they had decided to get a divorce. I knew that they argued a lot, but I never expected this.

Dad moved out of the house the next day. Oh man, did I hate to see my dad leave!

When he left, **I lost my family living in the same house together and all the fun times we had had together.**

Are you beginning to see that children can experience many **different types of losses**? Unfortunately, losses just seem to go with us everywhere we go.

- They go to school with us.
- They are by our side at home.
- They go out to play with us in the neighborhood.

Perhaps <u>you</u>, too, have already experienced one of the losses you have just read about. You might have even experienced a loss that was not mentioned.

Boys and girls, I wish I could tell you that every day of your life you would be receiving a blue ribbon for winning first place for an event happening in your life. It feels good to win, doesn't it?

But, I have to be honest with you and say that life is <u>not</u> going to be filled with blue ribbons and winning every day because -------

Losses are a <u>normal</u> part of life, even in the lives of children.(1)

Bubby says: None of us can win a blue ribbon everyday to hang on our wall at home, not even us rabbits. I have had lots of losses, too.

So, losses are a normal part of life, even in the lives of rabbits and children. How do I know that children have losses? There are many stories in the Bible that tells me that.

So, grab your Bible for the first story on your journey. This story is about a young boy whose name was Joseph. Boy, did he really have a lot of losses! Let's read it together.

Bible Story

Joseph and His Brothers
Genesis 37-50

Joseph was one of the 12 sons of Jacob and was born to him in his old age. To show his love for Joseph, Jacob made him a beautiful coat of many different colors. Of course, Joseph's brothers thought this meant that their father loved Joseph more, and they hated Joseph. They hated him so much that they couldn't say a kind word to him.

One day while Joseph's brothers were caring for their father's flock of sheep, Joseph's father said to him, "Your brothers are out in the field taking care of my sheep. I want you to take some food to them."

So, Joseph rode his camel out into the field in search of his brothers. When his brothers saw him coming, they made plans to kill him and tell their father that he had been eaten by a wild animal. But, Reuben, the oldest of the brothers said, "Let's not kill him. Let's throw him into a pit in the desert, and he'll eventually die without us touching him." Secretly, Reuben planned to come back later to rescue Joseph, and take him back to his father.

So, they stripped Joseph of his beautiful coat, which his father had made for him, and threw him into the pit. They then sat down to eat their dinner.

As they were eating, they looked up and saw a caravan of traders coming down the road. Their camels were loaded with things they were going to sell in Egypt. This gave one of the brothers an idea. "Let's sell Joseph to these traders. That way we can get rid of Joseph and make some money, too."

So when the traders came by, Joseph's brothers pulled him out of the pit and <u>sold him to the traders</u> for twenty pieces of silver. The traders continued on their journey to Egypt, taking Joseph along with them. Joseph was now <u>separated from his father, his home, and the country in which he was born.</u>

The brothers then killed a goat, spattered its blood on Joseph's coat, and took the coat to their father and asked him to identify it. "We found this in the field," they told him. "Is it Joseph's coat?"

Their father recognized it and began sobbing loudly. "A wild animal has eaten him. Joseph is probably torn into pieces."

Meanwhile, the traders arrived in Egypt with Joseph. They sold him to Potiphar, an officer in the court of Pharaoh, the King of all of Egypt.

The Good News is:

The Lord Was With Joseph

(Genesis 39:2 KJV)

One day when Joseph was a little older, Pharaoh made Joseph the Governor of Egypt. Years later, a worldwide famine broke out over all the earth and people were starving for food. Because the Lord was with Joseph, He had told Joseph in a dream that the famine was coming and to store up food before it came.

And that is exactly what the Egyptians did under Joseph's leadership as Governor. People in faraway lands heard that Egypt had food, and thousands of people began coming to Egypt begging to buy food.

As the people began arriving in Egypt to buy food, Joseph willingly helped those who were experiencing losses in their lives. How was he able to do this?

The answer to that is: Joseph's attitude and behavior had remained Christ-like, even though he had experienced losses in his life. He found ways to continue to enjoy life. One of the ways Joseph continued to enjoy life was by helping others in need.

What Can You Learn From This Story?

As you begin your own ***Journey of Healing***, there are 3 very important points you can learn from the life of Joseph that will help you when you experience a loss.

1. Just as the Lord was with Joseph when he experienced losses, He is also with you.

2. Joseph's attitude and behavior remained Christ-like in the midst of losses in his life.

3. Joseph helped others in need.

Memory Verse

The Lord was with Joseph

(Genesis 39:2)

A Prayer For You

Father God, as you were with Joseph during the time of his losses, I thank you that you are with every boy and girl who are experiencing a loss in their lives, too. May their attitude and behavior remain Christ-like, even in the midst of experiencing a loss. I also ask you to help them continue to enjoy life.

Chapter 2 Review

What Does Loss Mean?

Define Loss: A loss is a separation from someone or something of special value to you.

1. There are many different types of losses.

2. Losses are a normal part of life, even in the lives of children.

3. You can continue to be happy after a loss in your life.

4. Joseph, a young man in the Bible, experienced many different types of losses.

   - His brothers hated him because they thought their father loved him more

   - His brothers stole his coat of many different colors

   - His brothers threw him into a deep pit

   - His brothers sold him to traders going to a faraway country

   - He was separated from his father

   - He lost his boyhood home and the country in which he was born

5. Joseph's attitude and behavior remained Christ-like, in spite of losses in his life.

6. Joseph helped others in need.

7. Memory Verse: The Lord was with Joseph. (Genesis 39:2)

Chapter 2 Activities

What Does Loss Mean?

Directions: To begin your activities for this chapter, Bubby will give you a scripture, an exercise, and a tip that will help boost your self-esteem. Next, will be questions for you to answer on the Bible story. Be sure to take time to memorize the memory verse and pray your own personal prayer. Finally, you will answer questions and do activities to check your understanding of *What Does Loss Mean.*

 Hi, kids! Here I am to give you the first scripture to boost your self-esteem on your journey. Check it out in the box.

Self-Esteem means:

- How you feel about yourself
- The opinion you have of yourself
- How much value you place on yourself

> **GOD LOVES YOU**
> For great is Your love, higher than the heavens; Your faithfulness reaches to the skies. (Psalm 108:4 NIV)

1. Do you ever feel like nobody loves you? Do you sometimes not love yourself? Explain your thoughts on the lines provided.

   _____

   _____

2. How high is God's love for you? You can find the answer in the box above.

   _____

3. Discover more about God's love for you in the following scriptures.

   - Matthew 10:30 – He loves me so much He knows the number of _____ on my head.

   - Psalm 4:8 – He loves me so much I can lie down and sleep knowing He will keep me _____.

   - John 3:16 – He loves me so much He gave his _____ for me.

4. **Take a tip from me:** It is impossible to measure how wide, long, high, or deep God's love for you really is. Though you can't measure it, God wants you to experience His love for you in your life. So, the next time you have thoughts of feeling unloved, say out loud: "God's love for me is higher than the heavens." It will make you feel as though you can jump high enough to touch the stars!

Why not thank God for loving you so much by writing out the following prayer.

- **Thank you, God, for loving me so much.**

_____

_____

Joseph and His Brothers

5. Think about the Bible story of Joseph and His Brothers. Try naming the losses Joseph experienced as a young boy on the lines below.

_____   _____

_____   _____

6. Who does the Bible say was with Joseph when he experienced his losses? _____. (Genesis 39:2)

7. The Lord is with _____ when a loss occurs. (Write your name in the blank.)

8. Circle the word that describes Joseph's attitude and behavior during the time of his losses?   (Rude)   (Christ-like)

9. Was Joseph willing to help others who were experiencing losses in their life? Circle your answer. (Yes)   (No)

10. In the blank provided, write down the memory verse from the Bible story about Joseph and His Brothers and then memorize it.

   - **The Lord was with Joseph.** (Genesis 39:2)

   _____

11. Write a short prayer thanking God for being with you during times you experience losses. You might also ask Him to help you have a Christ-like attitude like Joseph did during times you experience losses.

   _____

   _____

   _____

What Does Loss Mean?

12. Now, let's see what you learned about losses. Start by writing the definition of loss on the lines below.

   - **A loss is a separation from someone or something that is of special value to you.**

   _____

   _____

   _____

13. Are losses a normal part of life? Circle the answer.   (Yes)   (No)

14. Name a way you can continue to be happy after a loss in your life?

   _____

   _____

15. Bubby experienced losses, too. The following pictures are of Bubby and some of the losses he has experienced. See if you can name his losses on the line provided.

(1) _____

(2) _____

(3) _____

(4) _____

16. Now, think about <u>your loss</u>. Draw a picture or write a story of a time you have experienced a loss.

Next Stop: Facts About Losses. Remember: God Loves YOU.

The Lord was with Joseph

Genesis 39:2

Additional Questions, Notes, and Drawings

Chapter 3

Facts About Losses

You are off to a good start on your **_Journey of Healing_**. You have learned the meaning of loss, how to recognize different losses, and have named a loss or losses you have experienced.

Probably the first thing you discovered about losing someone or something of special value to you was that it hurt really bad deep down inside of you, didn't it? Losses can sometimes make you feel as though a big bolt of lightning has hit you right down deep inside.

Let's learn more about what hurting inside means, as well as learn more facts about losses that will help you understand them better.

Fact # 1: All Losses Hurt Inside

When you are hurting inside, it means that your **feelings** are hurting. This type of hurt is different from a physical hurt. Often times a physical hurt can be seen and made to feel better quickly. For example, you might remember a time when you fell down and scratched your knee. No doubt the first thing you did was run into the house so your mom could put a band-aid on your bleeding knee to make it feel better. When your feelings are hurting way deep down inside of you, the hurt can't be seen, but you know it is there.

And yes, it hurts so badly that it feels like a big bolt of lightning has hit you inside.

Fact #2: Losses Are Not Your Fault

When losses occur, children often blame themselves and think it is their fault. For example: some children believe it is their fault when their parents divorce. They sometimes think that if they had been a better kid, maybe their mom and dad would not have divorced. Losses that you have no control over are not your fault. This means that there is nothing you could have done to have stopped the loss from happening.

Fact #3: Losses Cannot Be Replaced

Sometimes adults want to comfort and protect children by offering them a replacement for whatever they have lost.[1] For example: Suppose your pet died. Not wanting to see you hurting, your parents might want to replace your pet with another pet quickly. Of course, it is okay to get another pet, but the one you lost cannot be replaced. The same is true with any loss you might experience ---- it cannot be replaced.

Fact #4: Everyone Suffers Losses

There is no one who goes through life without having a loss of some kind. In fact, people of all ages experience losses: moms, dads, boys, girls, teenagers, and grandparents.

Fact #5: Losses Create Questions In Your Mind

When you have been separated from someone or something of value to you, it creates a lot of questions on your mind. Example: "Why do people die?" "If Mom and Dad no longer love each other, does that mean they don't love me either?" "Did my pet go to heaven when he died?" Your questions, concerning any loss you have experienced, deserve an answer. So, always ask any question on your mind.

Fact #6: Losses Bring Changes Into Your Life

When you experience a loss of any kind, it brings changes into your life. Your life will be different and not the same because the loss has changed it. For example: (1) Suppose a fire destroyed your home. You and your family would have to start all over again in another neighborhood without the things that once meant so much to you.[2] Suppose your best friend moved to another state. Your life would change because you would no longer have your friend nearby to do all the fun things the two of you once did together.

Experiences of our Journey Friends

Hadley

Before my dad died, I had only known one person to die and that was my grandpa. Grandpa was really, really old when he died, so I couldn't believe my dad died so young. I miss my dad so much.

I was also sad to see my mom so unhappy. I thought it was my responsibility to take care of her and make her happy. If she wasn't happy, I thought it was my fault.

The thing that changed the most for me when Dad died was all the fun things we did together. One of the funniest things that happened quiet often was when Mom baked a pie. We would see who would be the first one to steal the pie from the refrigerator. Guess what would happen then? The one who got the pie first would sneak up behind the other one and throw the pie in their face. Would we ever get in trouble with Mom for that!

Another fun thing we did together was tell silly jokes that would make us laugh and laugh.

At night after I did my homework, I'd play the piano and Dad would sit on the bench beside me and sing. We'd pretend we were having a concert. I miss hearing my daddy sing.

I had so many questions: "Where do people go when they die?" "Is Mom going to die, too?" "What about me, am I going to die?" My friends at school treated me differently after Dad died. "Why won't they talk to me," I wondered. "What can I say to them?"

Crystal

When Jay started bullying me, it changed the way I felt about myself. I felt so unloved and worthless. When I looked into the mirror, I no longer saw a pretty face. Jay said I was ugly, so I started to believe it. My grades in school began to change from A's to F's.

Every day I went to school thinking that I would tell my teachers what Jay was doing to me, but I was too scared to tell. "Why can't the other kids who see what Jay is doing help me," I wondered.

But, instead of helping me, some of them even joined in with Jay, and started making fun of me, too. They must have thought it was cool to make fun of another person. Someone I thought was my friend joined in, too. I guess she wanted to be with the in-crowd.

"What I have done to deserve this? Is it my fault?" I wondered.

Moving to another state brought a lot of changes into my life. I missed my best friend, Stacy. After school every day, we always played with our Barbie dolls in my playroom. On Friday nights, our moms would let us spend the night with each other.

I also missed special things I had done in my neighborhood, like the crawfish boils, 4ᵗʰ of July parties, and Christmas mornings. For crawfish boils, the street was blocked off on both ends and long tables were stretched out in the middle of the street with newspapers on them. Then boilers of crawfish were dumped onto the tables, and all the neighbors gathered around to eat.

On the 4ᵗʰ of July, my neighbor bought hundreds of dollars of firecrackers for the kids in the neighborhood to enjoy. On Christmas morning as soon as the kids were done opening presents from Santa Claus, we'd rush out to one another's house and show off our new toys. Every day on Deerlick Lane was special to me.

When my mom drove me to my new school the first day, I sat frozen to the seat of the car, and did not want to get out of the car to face all the new kids. My mom asked me, "Do you want me to go in with you to find your classroom?" I said, "No! The kids will think I am a baby having my mom come in the school with me."

While I sat there in the car, unable to get out, I wondered: "Why did Daddy make us move? Who is going to be my new friend?"

At last, I was able to get out of the car, and I moved slowly into a new world that I had never seen.

I cried and cried for days when my dog, Fala, died. My dad kept saying to me: "Don't cry. I'll buy you another dog at the pet store." I know that Dad was only trying to make me feel better, but I didn't want another dog; I wanted Fala back! I kept asking Dad, "Did Fala go to heaven?"

Zach

When my parents divorced, I thought it was my fault. Maybe they were mad at me for not cleaning my room and taking out the garbage. I kept thinking, "If I had been a better kid, they would have wanted to stay together."

The divorce brought so many changes into my life that it made my head swirl round and round. I now had two houses – Mom's house and Dad's house. My mom got custody of us kids, so we only got to see our dad every other weekend.

I missed all the fun things we did together. Spending the day at the zoo, family vacations, and family holidays were over for us as a family.

Man, do I wish I could get my parents back together again! I often wondered "What can I do to fix their problem?" I also wondered, "Since Mom and Dad no longer love each other, does that mean that they no longer love me?"

❋ ❋ ❋ ❋ ❋ ❋ ❋ ❋ ❋ ❋ ❋

As you can see, the kids traveling with you on your *Journey of Healing*, had a lot of things going on in their lives.

- Hadley thought it was her responsibility to take care of her mom after her dad's death.

- Crystal started to believe the rude things Jay said to her were true.

- Heather missed her old neighborhood, especially her friend Stacy, and longed for a friend at her new school.

- Hannah wanted her pet dog back, not a replacement for him.

- Zach thought that his parents' divorce was his fault.

Though each kid had a different loss and different things going on in their lives as a result of the loss, they all had certain things in common: they hurt inside, the loss brought changes into their lives, and they all had many questions on their mind that they wanted answered.

Perhaps you, too, have had some of the same thoughts and questions on your mind about your loss. Be sure to ask the adult traveling with you any question that you have. They are traveling with you on your *Journey of Healing* to help you.

Bubby says: You may be hurting inside from the loss you have experienced. It hurts to be separated from someone or something of special value to you. But I promise you that one day, the pain will begin to get better and the sunshine will shine in your life again.

Come to think of it, why not go out and have some fun with your friends today and let the sun shine down on you? It is okay to play and have fun even when you have experienced a loss. So hop to it!

Bible Story

God Hurt Inside

Genesis 3; John 3:16; Luke 4:18

The Bible tells about the first time that God experienced a loss and hurt inside. It happened like this:

When God created the first man and woman, Adam and Eve, they became His very special friends. He made the beautiful Garden of Eden to be their home. He placed animals in the garden, beautiful flowers and trees for them to enjoy, and plenty of fruits and vegetables for them to eat.

Also standing in the middle of the Garden of Eden were two trees called the Tree of Life and the Tree of Knowledge of Good and Evil. God made it clear to Adam and Eve that the whole garden was theirs to enjoy, but He had one rule for them to follow: "Do not eat from the Tree of Knowledge of Good and Evil."

Every day God walked in the garden to visit and talk with his close friends. One day when He came for a visit, He found out that they had disobeyed Him and had eaten the fruit from The Tree of Knowledge of Good and Evil.

Adam and Eve's sin separated them from God. God lost their friendship, as well as all the other people born into the world after them.

This loss of friendship made God hurt inside for the whole world.

Because God still loved people so much, one day He sent His son, Jesus, into the world to shed His blood to forgive their sins. This would give all people, including you and me, an opportunity to be friends with God again. Isn't that exciting?

But, God sent Jesus into the world to do something else, too. Take a look at what Jesus said God sent Him to do.

He has sent me to heal the broken-hearted.
(Luke 4:18 NKJV)

What Can You Learn From This Story?

Because God knows what it is like to experience a loss and hurt, He knows how you hurt when you experience a loss in your life also, and He wants to heal your broken heart.

Memory Verse

He has sent me to heal the broken-hearted.

(Luke 4:18)

A Prayer For You

Father God, I thank you that you are with each boy and girl whose heart is hurting. Thank you for sending your son, Jesus, into the world to forgive our sins, and to heal our broken hearts.

Chapter 3 Review

Facts About Losses

Define Loss: A loss is a separation from someone or something of special value to you.

1. Six Facts about Losses

    (1) All losses hurt inside.

    (2) Losses are not your fault.

    (3) Losses cannot be replaced.

    (4) Everyone suffers losses.

    (5) Losses create questions in your mind.

    (6) All losses bring changes into your life.

2. God experiences losses, too.

3. Because God knows what it is like to hurt and experience a loss, He feels your hurt, too.

4. Memory Verse: He has sent me to heal the broken-hearted. (Luke 4:18)

Chapter 3 Activities

Facts About Losses

Directions: To begin your activities for this chapter, Bubby will give you a scripture, an exercise, and a tip that will help boost your self-esteem. Next, will be questions for you to answer on the Bible story. Be sure to take time to memorize the memory verse and pray your own personal prayer. Finally, you will answer questions and do activities to check your understanding of *Facts About Losses*.

 Hi, kids! Do I ever have scriptures that will boost your self-esteem. Check them out in the box.

Self-Esteem means:

- How you feel about yourself
- The opinion you have of yourself
- How much value you place on yourself

GOD CALLS YOU SPECIAL NAMES
Friend- - John 15:15   Strong- -Ephesians 6:10
Bold- -1 John 4:17   Conqueror- -Roman 8:37

1. Has someone ever called you rude names? If so, what were they?

   _____   _____   _____

2. Have you ever called yourself names, such as stupid or ugly?

   _____   _____   _____

3. Write the special names God calls you listed in the box above.

   _____   _____

   _____   _____

4. Read the following scriptures and find other name's God calls you.

   - Matthew 5:13 _____   - Matthew 5:14 _____

   - Acts 1:8 _____   - 1 Peter 2:9 _____

5. **Take a tip from me:** Can you imagine being at a soccer game and hear God's voice on the sidelines hollering: "You are **bold**, you are **strong**, you are a **conqueror!**" "Good job, good job, my special **friend!**" Those names will give you so much confidence that you can win the soccer game and outrun me in a race!

Write out the following sentence thanking God for the special names He calls you.

• **Thank you, God, for calling me so many special names.**

_____

_____

God Hurt Inside

6. In the Bible story, God Hurt Inside, you read that God experienced a loss and hurt inside. What was the first loss God experienced?

_____

_____

7. Because God still loved people so much, one day He sent His son, Jesus, into the world to forgive man's sins so He could be friends with all of mankind again. Jesus said that God also sent Him into the world to do something for people whose hearts were hurting from losses in their lives.

Write down the memory verse showing the other reason Jesus came into the world.

• **He has sent me to heal the broken-hearted.** (Luke 4:18)

_____

_____

8. Write a short prayer asking God to heal your broken heart from the loss you have experienced while you are on this ***Journey of Healing***.

_____

_____

 **Facts About Losses**

9. Now, let's check out what you learned on Facts About Losses. Answer the following questions about each of the six facts.

Fact #1: All Losses Hurt Inside

Remember the loss you named in chapter 2 that you had experienced? Draw a picture of yourself. Then draw an arrow showing where you hurt the most because of your loss.(2)

Fact #2: Losses Are Not Your Fault

Do you ever feel that the loss you have experienced is your fault? If so, tell why.

_____

_____

_____

Fact #3: Replacing Losses

Can losses be replaced? Circle your answer.   (Yes)   (No)

Fact #4: Everyone Suffers Losses

Name someone you know who has experienced a loss and the loss that they experienced.

_____

Face #5: Losses Create Questions In Your Mind

List any questions you may have about the loss you have experienced.

_____

_____

_____

Fact #6: Losses Bring Changes Into Your Life

This question has two parts.

- On the following page, draw a picture or write a story about your life **BEFORE** your loss.

- On the next page, draw a picture or write a story about your life **AFTER** your loss to show how your life has changed as a result of the loss.

MY LIFE <u>BEFORE</u> MY LOSS

MY LIFE <u>AFTER</u> MY LOSS AND HOW IT CHANGED

Next Stop: On your next stop, we will explore **What Does Grieve Means**. Remember: God Calls YOU Special Names.

He has sent me to heal the broken-hearted.

Luke 4:18

Additional Questions, Notes, and Drawings

Chapter 4
What Does Grieve Mean?

Bravo!!! You have been doing so well on your ***Journey of Healing***. You are doing a great job working all the activities in each chapter, and learning so many new things about losses. In the last chapter, you learned some very important facts about losses that I believe will help you understand them better. On this stop, I'd like to ask you a few questions about some things that might be going on in your life as a result of your loss.

The first question I want to ask you is this: "When you first experienced your loss, did you suddenly feel **numb**?" Some kids have described it as feeling as though they were sleepwalking; others have said they felt as though they were walking around in a fog. It is normal to feel that way when you first experience a loss. You might say that "your feelings have disappeared" or "your feelings are gone," because you really don't feel anything.

The Bible tells the story about a man named Job who lost his family, servants, animals, and money in a short period of time. When his friends came to visit him, they sat on the ground and no one spoke a word, including Job, for seven days and nights. Wow! I'd say Job was numb, wouldn't you? (Job 2:13)

The second question I want to ask you is this: "After the numb feeling wore off, did you want to pretend as though the loss you had experienced did not happen at all?" That's normal if you did, but it is not a healthy thing to do. It is called **denial** or pretending something is not real.

May I let you in on a little secret? Grown-ups sometimes react this way, too. The reason kids and grown-ups want to pretend the loss never happened is that the pain of the loss hurts so badly inside that they don't want to even think about it. So, to keep from feeling that pain, they ignore the loss and stuff their feelings deep inside.

But, you know what? Stuffing feelings deeper inside of you causes more pain. Not only that, but it will usually cause your behavior to change from the way you normally act.

A change in behavior might include:

- withdrawing to your room, not wanting to see or play with anyone

- stop participating in activities at school that you once enjoyed

- begin fighting, yelling, and acting rude

- start acting sort of goofy trying to make people laugh to gain attention

- throwing temper tantrums

- have problems concentrating on your school work

- staying real busy, doing things to keep your mind off your pain

First, let me assure you that if you are experiencing any one of these different forms of behavior, you are not a bad kid. You are probably just sad about losing someone or something of value to you and do not know what to do about the pain of that loss.

So, some of the questions you might be asking now are: "What <u>am</u> I supposed to do about the pain I feel inside about losing someone or something special to me?" "What <u>can</u> I do to help my behavior go back to being the kind of kid I used to be before my loss?"

The answer to those questions is: **all losses must be grieved.** What exactly does that word **grieve** mean?

---

*Grieve means to
feel and express sadness.*

As you began to feel and express sadness over your loss, all those feelings you are having will come out in the open and won't be stuffed inside of you any longer. In time, the pain will start to heal. Not only that, but your behavior goes back to being the kind of kid that you were before your loss.

Experiences of our Journey Friends

When my daddy died, I went to the funeral, but I knew nothing about what was going on. It was like I was there, but I wasn't there. I felt like I was walking around in a daze. This numb feeling lasted about two weeks, and then I really started hurting, because I knew my dad was not coming back home to me. But, I didn't want to think about it, so I stayed **busy.** I stayed busy trying to do things to make my mom happy, so she wouldn't hurt so much. Other times, I played games on my computer for hours. Sometimes I even pretended like Daddy had not died.

Jay's bullying caused me to **withdraw** from everyone. Every day when I came home from school, I would lock myself in my room, and stay there until it was time for the evening meal. Often times, Dad would come to the door and try to get me to come out, but I refused. I didn't want to see anyone or play with anyone.

I was eleven years old when I had to move to a new city. I wanted friends so much, but nobody acted friendly toward me. I thought I could make friends by being funny. Anything I could do to make the other students laugh, I did it. I thought by **clowning around** it would get the student's attention, and they would then accept me. Besides, clowning around eased the pain I was experiencing inside from moving and not having any friends at my new school.

When my dog Fala died, I did not want to see or play with anyone. When I came home from school everyday, I went straight to my room, and closed the door. My mom and dad would knock on my door, trying to get me to come out. But, I only came out of my room to eat. **I stopped being a part of school activities that I enjoyed.** I was just so sad.

Zach

When Mom and Dad told me they were divorcing, I was not expecting it. The best way I can explain my first reaction to the news is by comparing it to playing in the snow or being out in the cold too long. Your nose, fingertips, and toes get all numb and you can't feel them because they are so cold. That's how I felt the night Mom and Dad told me they were divorcing.

Changes started taking place in my life. Our house was sold, my mom got custody of my brother and me. We went to live with my grandmother, and I only got to see my dad every other weekend.

My whole attitude changed. I began **fighting, yelling, and screaming** at everyone. I acted really rude to my mom and dad. I often **punched and hit** my little brother when my mom wasn't looking.

One day I even punched a boy out in the restroom at school. Guess where that landed me? You got it - - in the principal's office. I was suspended from school two days for fighting.

✳ ✳ ✳ ✳ ✳ ✳ ✳ ✳ ✳ ✳ ✳

As you can see, the kids traveling with us on our journey, not only experienced numbness after their loss, but their behavior also changed because they did not know what to do about the pain they were experiencing inside.

- Hadley stayed **busy**
- Crystal **withdrew**
- Heather acted like the **class clown**
- Hannah **stopped participating in school activities**
- Zach was rude to everyone; **fighting, yelling, screaming, punching**

From this point on in your journey, the special caring adult who is traveling with you on your journey will listen to you as you begin to feel and express the pain of your loss, rather than stuffing it. Your adult friend will also help you discover ways to express your feelings that you feel works best for you. As you do, all those feelings that you have had stuffed inside of you will come out in the open, and the pain of your loss will begin to heal.

Bubby says: Hey, kids! If you broke your leg, you know it would take a little time for your broken leg to heal, right? That's the way it is when you are hurting inside; it also takes a little time for your wounded heart to heal.

The good news is: As you began grieving your loss in a healthy way, you will begin to be happy and enjoy life once again!

Woohoo!! That should make you jump as high as me!

Bible Story
The Sermon on the Mount
Matthew 5:4

A large crowd of people always followed Jesus wherever He went. One day, as the crowds were following Him, He went up on a hillside with His disciples and sat down. The crowd gathered all around Him. Everyone knew that when Jesus spoke, He always had powerful words to teach them that would help in their daily lives.

On this particular day, Jesus was giving them a list of ways they could be happy in life. One of the things on that list was a way to continue to be happy after losing someone or something of special value to you. Take a look at what Jesus said to do.

"Blessed are those who mourn
for they shall be comforted."
(Matthew 5:4 NKJV)

Mourn and grieve have the same meaning. You learned that grieve means to feel and express sadness. In this verse, Jesus made a special promise of what He would do for people when they grieve. His promise was: **they shall be comforted. Comfort means to feel less sad.**

How will Jesus comfort those who grieve? Sometimes He sends a special friend to give you a hug and listen as you pour out your feelings. Other times He comforts you as you read the Bible. But, one thing you can always count on: He will always find the time and a way to comfort you.

You might recall the story in the Bible about a group of mothers bringing their children to Jesus. His disciples told the mothers to take their children away and not bother Jesus.

When Jesus saw what was happening, He was angry with His disciples. He said to them: "Let the children come to me. Don't stop them. For the Kingdom of God belongs to those who are like these children." Then He took the children into His arms, placed His hands on their heads, and blessed them. (Mark 10:14,16 NLT)

What Can You Learn From This Story?

Jesus experienced loses and hurt inside. His first hurt was when Adam and Eve sinned. In other stories, we see Him hurting when people rejected Him; when people were sick; when his best friend, Lazarus, died. He knew that His children would also hurt when they experienced losses like He did. So, He wants to comfort **you** when you hurt.

Memory Verse

Blessed are those who mourn for they shall be comforted.

(Matthew 5:4)

A Prayer For You

Father God, I thank you that, as each boy and girl begins to feel and express their thoughts and feelings they are having about their loss, You will comfort them.

Chapter 4 Review

What Does Grieve Mean?

Define Grieve: Grieve means to feel and express sadness

1. All losses hurt inside.

2. All losses must be grieved.

3. God promises to comfort you when you grieve.

4. God comforts you in different ways. Some of those ways are:

    *   He sends a special friend to listen as you pour out your thoughts and feelings.

    *   Other times He will comfort you as you read the Bible.

5. Memory Verse: Blessed are those who mourn for they shall be comforted. (Matthew 5:4)

Chapter 4 Activities

What Does Grieve Mean?

Directions: To begin your activities for this chapter, Bubby will give you a scripture, an exercise, and a tip that will help boost your self-esteem. Next, will be questions for you to answer on the Bible story. Be sure to take time to memorize the memory verse and pray your own personal prayer. Finally, you will answer questions and do activities to check your understanding of *What Does Grieve Mean.*

 Hi, kids! Do I ever have a scripture for you that show's what a valuable person you are. Check it out in the box.

Self-Esteem means:

- How you feel about yourself
- The opinion you have of yourself
- How much value you place on yourself

> **God Values You**
> "Let the children come to me. Don't stop them. For the Kingdom of God belongs to those who are like these children." Then He took the children into His arms and placed His hands on their heads and blessed them. (Mark 10:14, 16 NLT)

1. Do you sometimes feel like no one takes the time to listen to you? If so, explain your answer.

   _____

   _____

2. Do you feel like a failure when you fail a test in school? If so, explain.

   _____

   _____

3. **Take a tip from me:** God cares about your feelings and opinions, and always has time for you. You are never a failure in His eyes. Doesn't that make you want to shout how valuable you are to God for the whole world to hear? Write the following sentences on the lines provided. Then thank God that He values you so much.

(1) God cares about what I think, my opinions, and my feelings.

_____

_____

(2) God has time to listen to me.

_____

(3) I am never a failure.

_____

(4) Thank you God, because you value me so much.

_____

_____

The Sermon on the Mount

4. In the Bible Story about The Sermon on the Mount, Jesus told us what to do when we experience a loss. Write out the scripture and memorize it.

- **Blessed are those who mourn for they shall be comforted.**
  (Matthew 5:4)

_____

_____

5. Write out a prayer asking God to comfort you as you begin to grieve your loss.

_____

_____

What Does *Grieve* Mean?

6. Now, let's see what you learned about this word grieve. Start by writing out the definition in the blank provided.

   • **Grieve means to feel and express sadness.**

   _____

7. Think about a loss you have experienced. Do you remember feeling **numb** after experiencing that loss? Draw a picture or write a short story about that time in your life.

8. When that numb feeling wore off, did your behavior change? Did you begin acting in ways that you normally did not act? If so, choose from the following ways which best describes your behavior and draw a picture or write a story about what you did.

(1) Withdraw to your room

(2) Stop Participating in School Activities

(3) Fighting, Yelling, Acting Rude

(4) Class Clown

(5) Throwing Temper Tantrums

(6) Cannot Concentrate on School Work

(7) Staying Busy

9. You are not a bad kid if your behavior changed. You now know that when you experience a loss you should grieve. When you grieve, you feel and express your sadness over your loss. What is the promise Jesus gives to us when we grieve?

_____

10. Place a check mark beside the ways Jesus comforts those who grieve.

- He leaves you all alone.

- As you read the Bible, certain scriptures comfort you.

- He sends a special friend to listen to you pour out your feelings.

Next Stop: On your next stop you will begin **Recognizing Feelings** that you might have stuffed inside of you. Remember: God Values YOU.

The Sermon on the Mount - Coloring Page

**Blessed are those who mourn
for they shall be comforted.**

Matthew 5:4

Jesus Blessed Children - Coloring Page

Let the children come to me.
Don't send the children away.

For the Kingdom of God belongs to those
who are like these children.
Then He took them up in His arms and blessed them.

Mark 10:14, 16

Additional Questions, Notes, and Drawings

Helping Hurting Children: A Journey of Healing – Children's Workbook

Chapter 5
Recognizing Feelings

Here we are back on track with your **_Journey of Healing_**. In the last chapter, we talked about the word grieve. You learned that the word "**grieve**" means to **feel** and **express** sadness about a loss you have experienced. You also learned that when you feel and express sadness, all those thoughts and feelings you had about the loss come outside in the open. They are not stuffed inside of you any longer causing you to hurt more.

In this chapter, you will learn to recognize and name those feelings you might have stuffed inside of you.

Let's take a close look at what the word **feelings** (or emotions as they are sometimes called) means.

> *Feelings are our responses*
> *to events which happen in our lives.*

Feelings might best be described as our **inner self** being expressed as to what is happening around us or to us. Feelings work much like a smoke alarm. Smoke alarms sometimes prevent a house fire by providing a warning signal. When our feelings go off inside of us, they are alerting us to an event that has just happened in our life so we can respond to it.

Just for fun, let's try out your "feelings alarm" now. Suppose your mom walked into your room and announced, "Tomorrow we are going to Disney World on vacation." How would that make you feel?

Suppose your brother told you that he had lost your skateboard. How would that make you feel?

I'm guessing that you felt excited about going to Disney World, and angry that your brother had lost your skateboard.

In this chapter you will learn to recognize and name many different kinds of feelings. You will also learn important facts about feelings that will help you understand them better. So, let's get started.

Fact #1: There Are Many Different Kinds Of Feelings. Examples are:

Love	Peaceful	Sad	Hate
Happy	Disappointed	Lonely	Hope
Joy	Tired	Jealous	Fear
Confused	Angry	Shame	Surprised
Mischievous	Embarrassed	Worry	Guilty
Brave	Cheerful	Silly	Excited

Fact #2: Honesty Is The Key To Naming Feelings

Psalm 51:6 says: You desire honesty from the heart so you can teach me to be wise in my inmost being. (NLT) That means when the "feelings alarm" goes off inside of you, God wants you to be <u>honest</u> in naming the feeling you are having in your inner self. Perhaps you have had certain feelings before, but you wouldn't voice the feeling because you thought it was wrong to feel the way you were feeling. The feeling is never wrong; it's what we do with the feeling that can be wrong. If you are angry, say you are angry. If you are afraid, say you are afraid; if you feel happy, say you are happy. All feelings are okay.

Fact #3: Feelings Go Up And Down

Feelings can be compared to riding on a roller coaster. A roller coaster takes you up high on the tracks and then quickly drops you low on the tracks. That is the same way it can be with your feelings. One minute your feelings may be up high causing you to have a happy feeling; the next minute your feelings may be down low with a sad feeling.

Fact #4: Feelings Can Be Very Confusing

To be confused means something is puzzling or causing you not to understand something. The reason your feelings may seem confusing to you is that it is possible to have more than one feeling about the same loss. For example, you might have an older brother or sister graduating from high school. You could be happy that they have earned their high school diploma, but sad if they are leaving home for college. Or suppose you had a loved one in your family who had to spend time in jail. You could be real angry at your loved one for doing a wrong and being in jail, but still love them. An opposite feeling about the same event can be confusing, but it is normal.

Fact #5: All Feelings Are Okay; Wrong Behavior Is NEVER Okay

God created us with a mind, body, and feelings. He gives us feelings to respond to the things that happen to us. There is no right or wrong feeling, but wrong behavior is never okay. It is wrong to kick, punch, or be rude to someone even if you feel angry. Jesus had a wide range of feelings, but He never sinned. He <u>loved</u> children, he felt <u>anger</u> at the moneychangers at the Temple, and He was <u>sad</u> when his friend, Lazarus, died. We should always strive to be like Jesus, no matter what we feel.

❋ ❋ ❋ ❋ ❋ ❋ ❋ ❋ ❋ ❋ ❋

Experiences of Our Journey Friends

When my daddy died, I felt so mixed-up and **confused**. All I could think of was: "If Dad really loved me, why did he leave me?" "If God is so good, why did he take my dad away from me?" I felt **sad** that I had not told Dad everyday that I loved him. I felt **guilty** if I didn't make my mom happy all the time. My head was spinning round and round; I was so confused.

I was so **afraid** of Jay bullying me that I didn't even want to go to school, or go out in my neighborhood to play. I also felt so **angry** with him that I wanted to punch him in the face for what he was doing to me. I secretly wanted to hurt him as much as he was hurting me.

Heather

When my dad told me we were moving to a new city, I had two different feelings going on at the same time. One minute, I would be so **sad** about having to leave all my friends, especially my best friend, Stacy. But, I was also **excited** about getting a new house and meeting new people.

Hannah

When my mom told me that my dog Fala had died, I was so **sad**. I cried and cried for days. Everything around me seemed dark and gloomy.

Zach

When my parents told me they were divorcing, I had so many different feelings going on inside of me. One minute I had this awful feeling of **guilt** because I thought I was the one who had caused the divorce by not always obeying my parents.

Sometimes I would sit in my room and **worry** about so many things: "When would I see my dad?" "Will there be enough money for us to live on?" "What if Dad moved out of town and left me?"

After our house was sold, I had to move and go to another school. I was **afraid** of meeting new kids and not having friends. I was also **embarrassed** around other kids because I thought I had the only family who had split up.

I was **sad** because I would no longer have my family living in the same house. But, probably more than anything else, I was so **angry** with my parents for doing this to our family. When I got angry, I yelled and screamed at my parents. Actually, I began fighting, yelling, and screaming at just about everyone, especially my little brother. One time I got sent to the principal's office for hitting a kid at school.

I know this sounds crazy, but sometimes I was **happy** that my parents were divorcing. Now, I wouldn't have to hear them arguing all the time.

❋❋❋❋❋❋❋❋❋❋❋❋

As you can see, the kids on our journey with us experienced a variety of different feelings.

- Hadley was confused with questions and feelings that didn't make sense to her when her daddy died, plus she had a lot of feelings of guilt if she didn't make her mother happy.

- Crystal was fearful of Jay and also angry at Jay for bullying her.

- Heather had two different feelings going on that were totally opposite one another when she moved. She was excited and sad.

- Hannah was sad about her dog, Fala, dying.

- Zach sounded as though he was riding on a roller coaster. Up and down the track he went with feelings of guilt, worry, fear, embarrassed, sad, and anger. He even had happy feelings because he wouldn't have to hear his parents argue anymore.

All the kids had one thing in common: They were **honest** in naming their feelings, no matter what it was. Which kid do you think needs to change his behavior? If you guessed Zach, you are right. It is wrong to punch people and be rude, no matter what you may be feeling.

Bubby says: Just like you, every day of my life I am faced with things in my life that sets off my feelings alarm. As you can see in this picture, my feelings alarm is going off now. What do you think I am feeling?

_____

Bible Story

The Adventures of David

Psalm 51:6

The Bible tells the story of David, who experienced many adventures in his life starting when he was just a young shepherd boy.

One day, while tending his father's sheep, David killed a lion and a bear with his own hands. He also killed a huge giant, named Goliath, with only a slingshot.

When he became a man, he had more adventures. God appointed David to be King. The reigning king, Old King Saul, did not like that idea, and wanted David dead. David had to run for his life, so Saul couldn't find him. Often times, he hid in caves to keep King Saul from killing him.

When David finally became King, his life of adventure was not over. He had to fight many battles against the Philistine Army with only a sword and a shield.

Wow! I'd say that David led quite an adventuresome life, wouldn't you? Can you imagine what he was feeling when he came face to face with a lion and a bear?

What if you were about to face a huge giant like Goliath with only a sling shot in your hands for protection? Can you even imagine how you would feel having to hide in a cave to keep from being killed? Caves are fun to explore, but to have to hide in them to keep from being killed by a mad man would not be very much fun, would it?

Though David was a very brave young man throughout his adventures, his "feelings alarm" went off many times. The Book of Psalms records some of the many different feelings David had.

Let's check out some of David's feelings.

Anger   God, knock the teeth out of their mouths; Lord, tear out the young lions' fangs. (Psalm 58:6 HCSB)

Fear   Fear and trembling overwhelm me. I can't stop shaking. (Psalm 55:5 NLT)

Confused   Lord, how long will You continually forget me? How long will You hide Your face from me? (Psalm 13:1 HCSB)

Tired   I am worn out from sobbing. Every night tears drench my bed; my pillow is wet from weeping. (Psalm 6:6 NLT)

Joy   You have turned my mourning into joyful dancing. You have taken away my clothes of mourning and clothed me with joy. (Psalm 30:11 NLT)

Anxiety   O, Lord, I am calling to you. Please hurry! (Psalm 141:1 NLT)

Trust   The Lord is my light and my Salvation, so why should I be afraid? (Psalm 27:1 NLT)

As you can see from these scriptures, David's feelings went up and down like a roller coaster. When his feelings alarm went off, he recognized and named the feeling he was having because he knew that God wanted him to be honest, no matter what he felt.

Take a look at the following verse where David talks about being honest about naming his feelings.

You desire honesty from the heart so you can teach me
to be wise in my inmost being.

(Psalm 51:6 NLT)

What Can You Learn From This Story?

David experienced many different kinds of feelings. Because he desired to know truth in his inward parts, David was honest about naming each feeling he had and did not try to hide his feelings. He cried out with feelings of anger, fear, joy, love, and confusion, to name a few. That is what God wants you to do.

Memory Verse

You desire honesty from the heart so you can teach me to be wise in my inmost being.

(Psalm 51:6)

A Prayer For You

Father God, I pray that each boy and girl will recognize their feelings and be honest in naming their feelings just like David did.

Chapter 5 Review

Recognizing Feelings

Define Feelings: Feelings are our responses to events which happen in our lives. Feelings are our inner self being expressed.

Facts About Feelings

1. There are many different kinds of feelings.

2. Honesty is the key to naming feelings.

3. Feelings may go up and down like a roller coaster.

4. Feelings can be very confusing.

5. All feelings are okay; wrong behavior is never okay.

6. Memory Verse: You desire honesty from the heart so you can teach me to be wise in my inmost being. (Psalm 51:6)

Chapter 5 Activities

Recognizing Feelings

Directions: To begin your activities for this chapter, Bubby will give you a scripture, an exercise, and a tip that will help boost your self-esteem. Next, will be questions for you to answer on the Bible story. Be sure to take time to memorize the memory verse and pray your own personal prayer. Finally, you will answer questions and do activities to check your understanding of *Recognizing Feelings*.

 Hi, kids! The scripture in the box will make you look at yourself in the mirror and say "WOW!" Check it out.

Self-Esteem means:

- How you feel about yourself
- The opinion you have of yourself
- How much value you place on yourself

> **God Uniquely Designed You**
> Oh yes, You shaped me first inside, then out; You formed me in my mother's womb. I thank You, God. You're breathtaking! Body and soul! I am marvelously made! (Psalm 139:13-14 MSG)

1. Has anyone ever made a rude remark about your appearance? If so, write down what they said.

   _____

2. Is there something about your appearance you do not like?

   _____

3. **Take a tip from me:** Everyone has a different shaped nose, ears, eyes, and teeth. Some wear glasses, some have curly hair. Some people are tall, some are short. That is what makes you the beautiful girl or handsome boy that you are. Write the following sentence as a prayer of thanksgiving for the way God uniquely designed you.

   - **Thank you, God. I am marvelously made!**

   _____

   _____

The Adventures of David

4. In the blank provided, write the memory verse from the Bible story about The Adventures of David and memorize it.

   • **You desire honesty from the heart so you can teach me to be wise in my inmost being**. (Psalm 51:6)

   _____

   _____

5. Write a short prayer asking God to help you to always be honest in naming your feelings, just like David.

   _____

   _____

Recognizing Feelings

6. Now, let's see what you learned about Recognizing Feelings. Start by writing the definition of feelings on the lines provided.

   • **Feelings are our responses to events which happen in our lives.**

   _____

   _____

7. Do feelings stay the same all the time?   (Yes)   (No)

8. Is it okay to have different feelings about the same event?   (Yes)   (No)

9. All feelings are okay: _____   _____ is never okay.

10. Now, let's try out your feelings alarm. Suppose the following situations were happening to you. Write in the blank how you would feel.

(1)   Your soccer team won the game.

_____

(2)   You trip over a desk and fall down in front of the class.

_____

(3)   Your dad is getting a new job and you have to move to a new city.

_____

(4)   Your brother blames you for something you did not do.

_____

(5)   You are home alone and you hear a knock on the door.

_____

(6)   You fail a test.

_____

(7)   You lost your home and everything in it during a storm.

_____

(8)   Your best friend moved to another state.

_____

(9)   Someone calls you rude names.

_____

(10) Your friend had a slumber party and you were not invited.

_____

11. Sometimes our feelings show up on our faces. Just by looking at us, others might be able to tell what we are feeling. Name the feeling you see on the two faces below.

_____   _____

12. Now, let's have some fun drawing "feeling faces." Starting below and on the next two pages, draw a round circle above each feeling listed. Inside the circle, draw a face that best describes the feeling listed.

<u>Angry</u>   <u>Fearful</u>

Embarrassed

Worried

Bored

Surprised

Disappointed

Guilty

Confused   Love

Cheerful   Hate

 **Next Stop:** On your next stop you will learn **OKAY WAYS for Expressing Feelings** in order to have good behavior. Remember: God Uniquely Designed YOU.

The Adventures of David – Coloring Page

**You desire honesty from the heart
so you can teach me to be wise in my inmost being.**

Psalm 51:6

Additional Questions, Notes, and Drawings

Chapter 6
Expressing Feelings

Good job, good job! You did fantastic in the last chapter of recognizing and naming feelings. Did it give you a desire to express all those feelings you might have stuffed deep down inside of you for so long? If so, that is exactly what you are going to be doing in this chapter. You will be given an opportunity to express all your feelings about the loss you have experienced, plus learn ways to have good behavior at the same time.

First, think back to the Bible story of David and the many adventures he had in his life. Remember that David experienced many different feelings, such as: joy, anger, fear, sadness.

David learned early in life that God wanted him to be **honest** in naming each feeling he was experiencing in his inner most being.

And now we are going to see another interesting thing David learned to do about his feelings in the following verse.

> "I poured out my complaint before Him;
> I showed before Him my trouble."
>
> (Psalm 142:2 KJV)

The key word in this scripture is the word **POUR.** Pour means to flow freely.(1) Everything David was feeling inside, he poured out freely, rather than keeping it stuffed inside of him. You might say that David used his heart just like a water pitcher. He poured everything in it out to God, whether it was joy, sadness, bitterness, or fear.(2)

How did he pour his feelings out? The Book of Psalms tells us of several different ways David used to pour out his complaint unto the Lord. Sometimes he sang; sometimes he danced; many times he wrote out his feelings to God.

Just like David, God wants <u>you</u> to pour out your feelings about events that are happening in your life, too. Having said that, always remember a very important fact that you learned about feelings.

All feelings are okay; <u>wrong behavior is never okay.</u>

This means that, no matter what you feel, you must walk in God's image and make good choices.

So, that's what you are going to learn now in this chapter -- **OKAY WAYS** to pour out your feelings and have good behavior as you do so.

Let's take a closer look at those okay ways on the following page.

Okay Ways to Pour Out Your Feelings

1. It's OKAY to <u>Talk</u> to Someone You Trust

One of the best ways to pour out and express your feelings is by talking about them with people you trust. Talking to another person helps you get your feelings out in the open, and another person may also help you see the situation more clearly. They might also be able to help you find a solution to the problem. People you might want to talk to are:

- Your Parents
- School Guidance Counselor
- Children's Church Pastor

- Professional Counselor
- A Support Group
- Other Kids Who Have Experienced Losses

When you are talking to someone you trust, it is okay to tell them exactly how you feel. Perhaps you have had certain feelings before, but you wouldn't voice the feeling because you thought it was wrong to feel the way you were feeling. The feeling is never wrong; it's what we do with the feeling that can be wrong. Its okay to be honest and say such things as, "I'm angry!" "Why has this happened to me?" "This shouldn't have happened to me!"

2. It's OKAY to <u>Cry</u>

Sometimes boys think crying is sissy because they have been told, "Big boys don't cry." Girls are often called "Cry-Babies" when they cry. As a result of remarks like these, boys and girls might have a tendency to hold their tears inside, causing them to hurt even more. Crying is **NOT** sissy, nor are we Cry-Babies when we cry. In fact, it is okay for everyone to cry: moms, dads, grandparents, girls, boys, and teenagers. God gave us tears to flow. They are a way of expressing our feelings.

3. It's OKAY to <u>Write</u> Down Your Feelings in a Notebook

When things happen in your life (good or bad), writing down those feelings can help you see exactly what your feelings are. Besides, it gets your feelings outside of you and on paper. This allows you to read and think every feeling through before acting upon it.

4. It's OKAY to <u>Draw or Paint</u>

Perhaps you do not like to write, but you like to draw or paint pictures. Use your creativity to express your feelings through pictures.

5. It's OKAY to <u>Sing</u>

Do you like to sing? Try making up a song with words expressing how you feel about an event going on in your life or a loss you have experienced. Then sing your feelings out from way down deep within.

6. It's OKAY to <u>Play a Musical Instrument</u>

If you play the guitar, piano, or any other instrument, play it as though you were expressing exactly how you feel inside. You might even try composing the words to your own song, and then play it on your favorite instrument. Music is a wonderful way of expressing your feelings and getting them outside of your inward being.

7. It's OKAY to <u>Dance</u>

On a popular TV show called *Dancing with the Stars,* the judges often remark to the contestants, "I could tell you were FEELING the words to the music while you were dancing." Dancing is a beautiful way of expressing your inner feelings.

8. It's OKAY to <u>Act</u> Out Your Feelings in a Puppet Show

Did you ever secretly want to be an actor or actress? Here is your chance. Make a puppet, or buy one. Build a make-believe stage. You can become the star of your own show and act out all your feelings.

9. No matter what OKAY WAY or ways you choose to express your feelings, there are three additional ways that should always be made a part of your life in order to have good behavior.

(1) **Prayer:** Pray and ask God to help you with the feeling that might be causing you to have bad behavior.

(2) **Memorize Scriptures:** Memorize Bible verses on the feeling or feelings which are causing you to act out with bad behavior. Repeat it everyday until you have the feeling under control. For example: If you are very angry, memorize: Be angry and sin not. (Ephesians 4:26 KJV) If you are

having a lot of fear, memorize: Fear not for I am with you. (Isaiah 41:10 KJV)

(3) **Exercise:** Exercise is an excellent way to control your feelings, and it is also healthy for your body. When feelings of anger, fear, sadness, or worry seem to overwhelm you, take a walk or go for a ride on your bike. Watch those feelings come under control.

Experiences of our Journey Friends

Hadley

I love to **write**. After my dad's death, my mom bought me a notebook to write down my thoughts and feelings I was having about Dad's death. I call it my memory album. Sometimes I wrote poems about him and other times I wrote about special memories I had shared with him. Some days, I pretended as though I was writing a letter directly to Daddy. I would tell him what was going on in my life and how much I missed him. I even wrote letters to God telling Him how sad I was that Daddy had died.

Crystal

Jay had threatened to hurt me if I told anyone what he was saying and doing to me. I finally ignored his threats and **talked** to my mom. We then went to my school's guidance counselor to see what could be done about his bullying me at school. My mom and the guidance counselor let me tell my story of things Jay had done to me, and also listened while I told them how afraid I was of him.

I also like to **exercise**. Many times when I hurt so bad inside from the things that Jay had been saying and doing to me, I went walking and running with my mom. We also **prayed** while we were walking and running. This helped me to get all my feelings outside of me, and the walking and running helped my body stay healthy.

Heather

I love to **dance**. There were many days I felt so sad after my family moved to a new city. I had no friends at my new school or in my neighborhood to play with after school. So, I would go in my room, turn on my favorite music, and make up dance steps which expressed just how I felt. If I was sad, I made up a slow ballet dance that expressed my feelings. If I was angry, my dance steps changed to a different beat. Dancing helped me pour out all my feelings about my new move.

Hannah

One of my favorite things to do is **draw and paint**. I was so sad when my dog died. It would make me feel so much better when I drew pictures of Fala and the fun times we had together.

Zach

My mom found a **Support Group** for me to join for Children of Divorced Parents, which held meetings once a week. I met other kids in this group whose parents were also divorced. I finally realized that I wasn't the only kid who had parents who were divorced. Being in this group helped me to talk out my feelings with those who understood what I was going through.

Often times the adult leader of our group would arrange for us to have **puppet shows** to act out exactly how we were feeling. Boy, did my angry feelings really come out then!

I also talked to my **children's church pastor** about the guilty feelings I was having, thinking I had caused my parents' divorce.

✳ ✳ ✳ ✳ ✳ ✳ ✳ ✳ ✳ ✳ ✳ ✳

God made each of us different and because of that, we express our grief in different ways, just like the kids on the journey with us:

- Hadley poured out her feelings by writing

- Crystal by talking and exercising

- Heather by dancing

- Hannah by drawing and painting

- Zach by joining a support group, acted out his feelings in puppet shows, and he also talked to his children's church pastor

And that's what you should do. You are a very unique person. God has designed you to pour out your feelings in a way that is best for you, and still have good behavior.

So, begin thinking of ways you are going to do this when you get to the activities.

Bubby says: Did you know that every rabbit is different? I bet you thought we all looked the same, didn't you? No sirree! We are all different and unique. We even express our feelings in different ways.

Right now, I am thinking of okay ways to express my feelings about the losses that I have had in my life. I have had them stuffed inside of me for a long time. I am so ready to get them out of me and have good behavior, too.

Bible Story
Cain Kills His Brother Abel
Genesis 4:1-8

This is the story of two brothers whose names were Cain and Abel. When Cain grew up, he became a farmer. When Abel grew up, he became a shepherd and took care of his dad's sheep.

One day Cain and Abel brought gifts to God to thank Him for all the good things He had done for them. Cain brought some of the things he had grown on his farm. Abel brought the best lamb born from one of his sheep.

God knows everything about us, and He knew the thoughts of both Cain and Abel when they brought their gifts to Him. God knew Abel really wanted to please Him, and give Him his best, so He was happy with Abel's gift, and accepted it. But, God knew that Cain did not give Him his best gift from his farm. God wasn't happy with Cain's gift, and did not accept it.

That made Cain so angry. God saw the look on Cain's face and said to him: "Why are you so angry, Cain? You will be accepted if you <u>respond</u> in the right way. But, if you refuse to <u>respond</u> correctly; then watch out. Sin is waiting to attack and destroy you, and you must control it." (Genesis 4:6-7 NLT)

But, Cain didn't listen to God. Even though God loved both brothers very much, Cain thought God loved Abel more than him. So, he began thinking bad thoughts about his brother. The longer he thought those bad thoughts, the angrier he became.

Helping Hurting Children: A Journey of Healing – Children's Workbook

One day he said to his brother, "Abel, come with me out into the fields." Because Abel loved his big brother and trusted him, he went out into the fields with him. When Cain got Abel out where nobody could see or hear them, he took a rock and killed his brother.

How sad that Cain did not respond as David when he expressed his feelings. Remember what the Bible said that David did?

"I poured out my complaint before Him;
I showed before him my trouble."

(Psalm 142:2 KJV)

What Can You Learn From This Story?

When Cain's feelings alarm went off inside of him, he did <u>not</u> express his feelings in a Christ-like way, and murdered his brother, Abel. Cain responded with wrong behavior. He should have poured out his complaints to God, in one of the Okay Ways like David did when his feelings alarm went off.

Memory Verse

I poured out my complaints before Him; I showed before Him my trouble.

(Psalm 142:2)

A Prayer For You

Father God, I thank you for giving each boy and girl feelings. Help them to express the feelings they are having in a way that is pleasing to you.

Chapter 6 Review

Expressing Feelings

Define Feelings: Feelings are our responses to event which happen in our lives. Feelings are our inner self being expressed.

Okay Ways to Express and Pour out Feelings

1. Talk to Someone You Trust, such as:

   - Your Parents

   - School Guidance Counselor

   - Children's Church Pastor

   - Professional Counselor

   - A Support Group

   - Other Kids Who Have Experienced Losses

2. Crying

3. Writing

4. Drawing or Painting

5. Singing

6. Playing a Musical Instrument

7. Dancing

8. Acting Out Feelings Using Puppets

9. Prayer, Memorize Scriptures, Exercise

10. Memory Verse: I poured out my complaint before Him; I showed before Him my trouble. (Psalm 142:2)

Chapter 6 Activities

Expressing Feelings

Directions: To begin your activities for this chapter, Bubby will give you a scripture, an exercise, and a tip that will help boost your self-esteem. Next, will be questions for you to answer on the Bible story. Be sure to take time to memorize the memory verse and pray your own personal prayer. Finally, you will answer questions and do activities to check your understanding of *Expressing Feelings*.

 Hi, kids! Now, here is a scripture that will help you do away with bad thoughts about yourself. Check it out in the box.

Self Esteem means:

- How you think about yourself
- The opinion you have of yourself
- How much value you place on yourself

> **God Desires that YOU Think Good Thoughts**
> Fix your thoughts on what is true, honorable, right, pure, lovely, and admirable. Think about things that are worthy of praise. (Philippians 4:8 NLT)

1. Do you ever have negative thoughts about yourself? If so, write down those thoughts in the blanks provided.

   _____

   _____

2. Replace those negative thoughts about yourself with good thoughts.

   _____

   _____

3. **Take a tip from me:** Thinking negative thoughts about yourself can become very depressing. The next time you have a negative thought, replace it with the way you are learning God sees and feels about you. It will make you feel good about yourself even on a cloudy day. Write out the following sentence thanking God that He desires for you to think good thoughts. You might also ask Him to help you do this.

- **Thank you, God that your desire for me is to think good thoughts about myself. Help me to always replace negative thoughts with good and lovely thoughts.**

_____

_____

Cain Kills his Brother, Abel

4. In the blank provided, write the memory verse showing what David did about his feelings, and memorize it.

- **I poured out my complaint unto the Lord. I showed before Him my trouble.** (Psalms 142:2)

_____

_____

5. Explain what the word **Pour** means in the above scripture.

_____

6. Did Cain pour out his feelings in one of the OKAY WAYS?   (Yes)   (No)

7. What happened when Cain responded with wrong behavior?

_____

_____

8. Write a short prayer asking God to help you pour out your feelings in a healthy and Christ-like manner.

_____

_____

Expressing Feelings

9. Just to be sure you remember exactly what the definition of feelings is, why not write it one more time on the lines provided.

   • **Feelings are our responses to events which happen in our lives.**

   _____

   _____

10. Now, let's see what you learned about Expressing Feelings from this lesson. Place a big ☑ check mark beside the OKAY WAYS to pour out your feelings and still have good behavior.

   ☐ Crying   ☐ Slamming Doors

   ☐ Drawing or Painting   ☐ Dancing

   ☐ Punching Someone   ☐ Writing

   ☐ Taking to Someone You Trust   ☐ Yelling at Your Parents

   ☐ Singing   ☐ Playing a Musical Instrument

   ☐ Throwing Objects   ☐ Having a Puppet Show

   ☐ Kicking Objects   ☐ Prayer, Memorizing Scripture, Exercise

11. Have you been using ways to express your feelings that are <u>not</u> okay? If so, on the next page write down the wrong ways you used. Or you might want to draw pictures showing how you expressed your feelings.

   Don't be afraid to tell or draw about wrong behavior you might have used in expressing your feelings. You are now learning OKAY WAYS to replace the old. This exercise is just to let you see the old you, and then you will see how you have changed your behavior. Isn't that neat?

My Old Ways of Expressing my Feelings

12. Pour Out Your Feelings

Now it is time to pour out your complaints and feelings about your loss or losses, but it must be done in the right way using good behavior. The following pages are "your own special place" where you can do that in your own unique way.

Follow these instructions.

(1) Use any of the **OKAY WAYS** you learned about in this chapter that is best suited for you. A chart, listing the Okay Ways, is on each page to help you remember.

(2) You probably will not pour out ALL your feelings in one day. That is okay. As you think of new feelings, come back to your special place, and pour out your feelings in your own unique way.

(3) Some days you might feel sad; some days you might feel angry; sometimes you may feel joyful. Whatever you are feeling, pour it out.

(4) If you choose to pour out your feelings in ways other than writing or talking, make a note of it on the page. It is like keeping a diary of how and when you poured out your feelings.

(5) Always remember that God gives us so much to be thankful for, even in the times we are experiencing a loss. So, try to make a practice of giving **THANKS** to God everyday, even on those days you feel sad.

(6) Are you ready to begin pouring? If so, talk to your adult friend traveling with you. They will be able to help you make the choice about the way or ways that is best suited for you.

Okay Ways to Pour out my Feelings

- ➤ Talk to someone you trust
- ➤ Crying
- ➤ Writing
- ➤ Drawing or painting
- ➤ Singing

- ➤ Playing a musical instrument
- ➤ Dancing
- ➤ Acting out with puppets
- ➤ Prayer, Memorize Scriptures, Exercise

I poured out my feelings - - (Psalm 142:2)

Okay Ways to Pour out my Feelings

- Talk to someone you trust
- Crying
- Writing
- Drawing or painting
- Singing
- Playing a musical instrument
- Dancing
- Acting out with puppets
- Prayer, Memorize Scriptures, Exercise

I poured out my feelings - - (Psalm 142:2)

Okay Ways to Pour out my Feelings

- Talk to someone you trust
- Crying
- Writing
- Drawing or painting
- Singing

- Playing a musical instrument
- Dancing
- Acting out with puppets
- Prayer, Memorize Scriptures, Exercise

I poured out my feelings - - (Psalm 142:2)

Okay Ways to Pour out my Feelings

➤ Talk to someone you trust
➤ Crying
➤ Writing
➤ Drawing or painting
➤ Singing

➤ Playing a musical instrument
➤ Dancing
➤ Acting out with puppets
➤ Prayer, Memorize Scriptures, Exercise

I poured out my feelings - - (Psalm 142:2)

Next stop: On your next stop, you will take a big step and learn to Forgive Others. Remember: God Desires that YOU think Good Thoughts!

"I poured out my complaint before Him;
I showed before him my trouble."

Psalm 142:2

Cain Kills His Brother Abel - Coloring Page

** **Remember:** Cain did not pour out his feelings in one of the Okay Ways and murdered his brother.

Why are you so angry, Cain?
If you refuse to respond correctly; then watch out.
Sin is waiting to attack and destroy you. You must control it.

Genesis 4:6-7

Additional Questions, Notes, and Drawings

Chapter 7
Forgiving Others

You've come a long way on your _**Journey of Healing**_. You started out on your journey by recognizing losses and naming a loss or losses that you have experienced. In the last two chapters, you learned how to recognize and express feelings about the loss you have experienced. You really deserve a pat on the back for all the hard work you have done on the activities in each chapter, especially getting all those feelings out from down deep inside of you. Doesn't that feel good?

Now, you have reached a very important stop on your journey and that is **Forgiving Others**. You might be wondering what forgiving others has to do with the loss you have experienced. The best way I know how to answer that question is in the following way.

All of the people that God created are connected in some way. We are connected by family, friends, and by many other people we meet on a daily basis. That means that, more than likely, there will be someone in our life who might hurt us in some way.

Rather than holding a grudge against them, we should forgive them for any pain they might have caused us, or we think they have caused us.

That's what God did when He experienced a loss. Let's review something you learned about God in a previous chapter.

Do you remember in Chapter 3, you learned that Adam and Eve's sin separated them from God and God lost their friendship?

The loss of their friendship caused God to hurt inside. But, because God still loved people so much and wanted to be friends with them again, He sent His son, Jesus, into the world to shed His blood and forgive all mankind for their sins.

What exactly does that word **forgive** mean?

> ## Forgive means to erase

No doubt you have seen your teacher at school erase the whiteboard at the end of the day. As she did, everything that she had written on the whiteboard was gone. It could no longer be seen.

That is exactly what happened when Jesus shed His blood on The Cross for us. He erased all of our sins.

Can you believe that while Jesus was hanging on The Cross over 2,000 years ago, you were on His mind? Isn't that awesome?

What Jesus did for you and me that day was a free gift. It did not cost us anything. When we accept his free gift and ask Him into our hearts to be our Savior, we get to go to heaven and be with Him forever and forever.

What Jesus gave us freely, He tells us in His word to do the same for others. Take a look.

**Remember, the Lord forgave you,
so you must forgive others.**

(Colossians 3:13 NLT)

Now that you know that **forgive** means to erase, let's look at some additional facts about forgiveness. Perhaps these facts will help you have a better understanding of what it means.

1. Forgiveness is a choice, not a feeling

Often times you might hear someone say: "They were so mean to me; I don't feel like forgiving them." Think of it this way. When your teacher assigns you homework, do you really **feel** like doing it? You probably do not. However, you make the choice to do it anyway because it is the right thing to do. That's the way it is with forgiveness. Always make the choice to forgive and erase a grudge you are holding against someone who has hurt you whether you feel like it or not.

2. People do not have to tell you they are sorry before you forgive them

Sometimes you might want to delay forgiving others because they haven't come to you and said, "I'm sorry." It would be nice if the person who hurt you told you he was sorry, but whether he does or not, forgive him anyway. As Jesus was hanging on the cross, the crowd was shouting, "Crucify Him! Crucify Him!" Jesus prayed, "Father, forgive them for they know not what they do." Jesus placed no conditions on the ones who were hurting Him before forgiving them. Nor did He wait for them to come to Him and ask His forgiveness. He chose to forgive. He chose to do the will of His Father who sent Him to shed His blood on the cross for the forgiveness of our sins. (Luke 23:34)

3. You may never forget the things people have done that hurt you

Often times, someone will say: "How can I forgive when I can't forget what they have done to me?" Think of it this way: Our minds are not like the delete key on a computer. If you make an error when you are typing on your computer, all you have to do is hit the delete key, and the error is erased. Our minds are not like that. But, when we make the choice to pass forgiveness on to others the way Jesus did for us, the hurt will no longer **sting** us like it once did.

✳ ✳ ✳ ✳ ✳ ✳ ✳ ✳ ✳ ✳ ✳

Let's check in with our Journey Friends and see what they are saying about forgiving others.

Experiences of our Journey Friends

Hadley

After my daddy died, there were times I was so angry with him. I was actually holding a grudge against him for leaving me. I thought, "If Daddy really loved me, he wouldn't have left me." Guess who else I was secretly holding a grudge against? Can you believe I was holding a grudge against God, too, for letting my dad die? But, I thought if I didn't tell anybody that I was holding a grudge against God that God wouldn't know it either. Isn't that funny? God knows everything.

It is a part of my life everyday. I just cannot forget about it.

Crystal

Jay thought that he was a big shot in the sixth grade, and I was just a little girl he could push around and call ugly names. "Why should I forgive him for something that was wrong for him to do in the first place?

And besides, **Jay has never told me he was sorry for hurting me.**"

Heather

When my family moved, I wanted friends so much at my new school and church. But, nobody seemed to like me, and a couple of girls were actually rude to me. Though I eventually started making friends, I still remember how rude these two girls were to me. I would never treat a new kid in school the way they treated me!

"I just don't feel like forgiving them."

Zach

I will always remember the night my parents told us that they were divorcing. I will always remember how my life was suddenly changed overnight. How can I ever forgive my parents for splitting up our family?

"Besides, it is a part of my life every single day, so I can't just forget about it."

❈ ❈ ❈ ❈ ❈ ❈ ❈ ❈ ❈ ❈

It looks as though Hadley, Crystal, Heather, and Zach had problems passing on to others the forgiveness that Jesus has given them.

- Hadley was holding a grudge against her daddy for dying and leaving her. She was also holding a grudge against God, too.

- Crystal was absolutely right! It was wrong for Jay to bully her. There is no excuse for him treating her that way, and he may never tell her he is sorry for bullying her. But, whether he ever tells her he is sorry or not, Crystal must learn to forgive.

- Heather is letting her feelings get in the way of passing on forgiveness to the two rude girls at her school. Forgiving them is going to be something that she should decide to do whether she feels like it or not.

- Zach will never forget that his parents got a divorce; after all, they all do not live in the same house anymore. Zach must learn that the divorce will always be a part of his life; it cannot be erased and forgotten. But through forgiveness, Zach can learn to live with it without bitterness.

Bubby says: Hey kids, think of forgiveness this way: It is sort of like playing basketball. You can't hold onto the ball to win; you must pass it on to your teammate. So, don't hold onto grudges; pass forgiveness on to someone who has hurt you, and **you will be a winner!**

Bible Story

The Unforgiving Servant

Matthew 18: 21-35; Colossians 3:13

There was a king who wanted to settle his accounts with his servants. One servant was brought to the king who owed him a very large sum of money. But, the servant could not pay, so the king issued an order to have his wife, children, and all that he owned be sold to repay the debt.

When the man heard what the king was going to do to him, he went to the king and fell on his knees before the king, begging. "Please be patient with me," he begged. "Give me a little more time and I will pay you the money I owe you."

However, the king had pity on him and said: **"Instead of giving you more time to pay me back, I'm going to forgive you of the debt. I'm going to erase the debt you owe me."**

Can you imagine how happy the man was that he did not have to pay back the money he owed to the king?

But, guess what? Someone owed this man a smaller amount of money. Unfortunately, the man could not pay him and said: "Please be patient with me, give me a little more time, and I will pay you the money I owe you."

What do you think he did?

Would you believe the man said: "No, I want my money. Hand it over to me now!"

Sadly, he chose not to do for someone else what had been done for him. He chose not to do as the Bible tells us to do.

Remember, the Lord forgave you, so you must forgive others. (Colossians 3:13)

When the king heard about this, it made him so angry. "I forgave my servant a large sum of money he owed me; I erased his debt," he exclaimed! "Now he refuses to forgive and erase the debt of the man who owes him money!"

So, the king had his unforgiving servant thrown in jail and he was tortured day and night for not passing on forgiveness.

What Can You Learn From This Story?

The unforgiving servant refused to erase a debt someone owed him, even though the king had erased his debt. When we don't forgive others, we hurt ourselves, our relationship with others, and we also hurt our relationship with God.

Memory Verse

Remember, the Lord forgave you, so you must forgive others.

(Colossians 3:13)

A Prayer For You

Father God, I ask you to help each boy and girl to forgive others who have hurt them, just as you have forgiven them.

Chapter 7 Review

Forgiving Others

Define Forgiveness: to erase

1. Additional facts about forgiveness:

   - Forgiveness is not a feeling; it is a choice.

   - People do not have to tell you they are sorry before you forgive them.

   - You may never forget some of the things that others have done that has hurt you. But, when you pass forgiveness on to others like Jesus did, the hurt will no longer sting and hurt you like it once did.

2. Holding grudges hurts us, our relationship with others, and our relationship with Jesus.

3. Memory Verse: Remember, the Lord forgave you, so you must forgive others. (Colossians 3:13)

Chapter 7 Activities

Forgiving Others

Directions: To begin your activities for this chapter, Bubby will give you a scripture, an exercise, and a tip that will help boost your self-esteem. Next, will be questions for you to answer on the Bible story. Be sure to take time to memorize the memory verse and pray your own personal prayer. Finally, you will answer questions and do activities to check your understanding of *Forgiving Others*.

 Hi, kids! Do I ever have a scripture for you to help you make good choices. I need this one also. Check it out in the box.

Self-Esteem means:

- How you feel about yourself
- The opinion you have of yourself
- How much value you place on yourself

> **God Gives YOU Courage**
> Be strong and of good courage, do not fear nor be afraid of them; for the Lord your God, He is the One who goes with you. He will not leave you nor forsake you. (Deuteronomy 31:6 NKJV)

1. Have you ever felt pressured to "follow the crowd," even when you knew it was wrong? Write down the times this has happened to you.

   _____

   _____

2. **Take a tip from me**: You are faced with making choices and decisions daily. You get to choose whether to be obedient to your parents and teachers or not. You get to choose to do what is right or to follow the crowd. Every time you take responsibility for your own actions, and make a choice to do what is right, it builds up your self-esteem. Write down the following prayer thanking God for giving you courage to make good choices.

   - **Thank you, God, for giving me courage to make right choices and decisions.**

   _____

   _____

3. In the blank provided, write down the memory verse telling us what God wants us to do about Forgiving Others and then memorize it.

   • **Remember, the Lord forgave you, so you must forgive others.**
     (Colossians 3:13)

   _____

   _____

4. Think about the man who could not pay a debt he owed, but the King erased and forgave him of his debt. Did he remember to do the same for the man who owed him money?   (Yes)   (No)

5. What did the King do to him for not forgiving the man his debt?

   _____

6. As you can see from this lesson Jesus forgave and erased all our sins on The Cross. However, there's a step we must take in order to be in heaven with Him one day. That step is asking Jesus to come into our heart to be our Savior.

   If you have never received God's free gift of forgiveness by accepting his son Jesus as your Savior, why not pray the following prayer with someone today.

   Prayer:

   I thank you God for sending your son, Jesus, into the world to forgive me of my sins. Jesus, I thank you for shedding your blood for me. I now ask you to forgive me of my sins. Come into my heart and be my Savior. In Jesus name, I pray. Amen.

   What is the date you prayed this prayer?_____

Forgiving Others

7. Now, let's see what else you learned about forgiveness. Start by writing the definition of forgiveness on the lines below.

   • **Forgiveness means to erase**

   _____

8. Is forgiveness a choice or a feeling? _____

9. Does the person who has hurt you have to say "I'm sorry" before you forgive them?   (Yes)   (No)

10. Does forgiveness mean you will forget the event that happened to you?
    (Yes)   (No)

11. When we choose not to forgive others as Jesus did for us, we hurt ourselves. Who else do we hurt?

    _____   _____

12. Is there someone in your life you are holding a grudge against and haven't forgiven? If so, be honest and name the person or persons in the blanks.

    _____   _____

13. Are you ready to give the gift of forgiveness to those who have hurt you? If so, try the following exercise using the next two pages.

    • Draw a whiteboard like the one in your classroom at school.
    • Write on the whiteboard the names of the people who have hurt you and what they did to you.
    • Then draw a picture of you holding a big erasure in your hand. Pretend you are erasing all the wrong things they have done to you.

My Whiteboard of Forgiving Others

My Whiteboard of Forgiving Others

 **Next Stop:** On this stop, you made a choice to Forgive Others. That is awesome. On your next stop, you will learn all about **Asking Others to Forgive You**. Remember: God Gives YOU Courage.

Jesus' Death on the Cross – Coloring Page

**Remember, the Lord forgave you,
so you must forgive others.**

Colossians 3:13

The Unforgiving Servant – Coloring Page

The Unforgiving Servant
The Man Who Chose not to Forgive Others

Matthew 18: 21-35

Additional Questions, Notes, and Drawings

Chapter 8

Asking Others to Forgive You

In the last chapter, you learned all about Forgiving Others who had hurt you. Then in your activities, you actually erased those hurts that others had caused you. Doesn't it feel so good to get rid of those grudges you might have been holding against others?

Now, let's talk about times that **YOU might have hurt others.** "Me? What did I do wrong?" you might be asking.

May I let you in on a little secret -- no one is perfect. We all make mistakes, and do things that are wrong. But, we should always be ready to confess our sins to God, and then be willing to ask others to forgive us for the things we have done to hurt them.

Unfortunately, a lot of times children have a hard time asking others to forgive them, or just simply saying the words, "I'm sorry." Some of the reasons they find it so hard to say those two words are:

1. Some are **embarrassed** to say the words, "I'm sorry."

2. Some think that saying "I'm sorry," is **a sign of weakness** and that others could take advantage of them if they say "I'm sorry."

3. Some refuse to apologize because they make a promise to themselves that they will **never do the same wrong again.** But, not doing the wrong in the future will not erase the wrongs of the past. Wrongs must be made right by apologizing to those who have been hurt.

4. Some say to themselves, **"I'll apologize later."** Most of the time, later never comes. Always be quick to apologize.

5. Sometimes, it is even hard to say "I'm sorry" to God. Some kids **feel that God will get mad with them when they do something wrong**, so they will try to hide their wrongs from Him.

Experiences of Our Journey Friends

Zach

I know I should not have used my brother for a punching bag during the time of our parent's divorce, but I was upset. I made a promise to myself that I would never hit him again. I also straighten my behavior up at school after I got sent to the principal's office for punching a kid in the nose. So, I didn't think that I needed to apologize. I was also rude to my parents but, I'm just a kid -- I'm not perfect. I was sure everyone could see that my behavior had changed and I was acting like the good kid I was before my parents divorced.

❈ ❈ ❈ ❈ ❈ ❈ ❈ ❈ ❈ ❈ ❈ ❈

It is true Zach had a terrible time when his parents divorced, but that did not give him the right to hurt others. Nor did it give him the right to not ask others to forgive him even though his behavior changed.

Bubby says: Saying "I am sorry" is one of the biggest things you will ever do.

Bible Story

The Prodigal Son

Luke 15:11-24

A man had two sons. The young son loved money and wanted more of it to buy things. He also wanted to travel and see the world, as well as to be his own boss. So, the young man made a bad choice.

He went to his father and asked him to give him the inheritance that would be his when his father died. Even though the father was sad that his son wanted to leave home, he gave him his share of the family fortune and the young man left home.

He traveled all around the world. He visited all of the places he had always wanted to visit and did whatever he wanted to do. He was happy that no one was telling him what to do. Since the young man had a lot of money, if he saw something he wanted, he bought it.

After a while, the young man ran out of money. He didn't even have enough money to buy food. He was so desperate and in need of money that he went to work for a man feeding his pigs. Can you imagine feeding muddy, fat, stinking old pigs? (Ugh!)

One day he looked at the filthy pig pen that he was working in and began to think about his father and the warm home he had left behind. "I will return to my father and tell him that 'I **am sorry**', and ask him to give me a job as one of his servants."

Perhaps he remembered the following scripture his father had taught him when he was a kid.

**Create in me a clean heart, O Lord,
and renew a right spirit within me.**

(Psalm 51:10 KJV)

So, he headed down the long road home to tell his father he was sorry, and how much he wanted to change his behavior.

When his father saw him coming down the road, he ran to meet him. Do you think the father was willing to take him back? Yes, but not as a servant. He welcomed him back home as his son, and forgave him for his bad choices.

What Can You Learn From This Story?

This young man made a poor choice. His behavior hurt him, as well as his father. We can learn through him that we should always be willing to look at our own lives for ways we have hurt others, ask God to forgive us, and then ask Him to give us courage to ask others to forgive us.

Memory Verse

Create in me a clean heart, O Lord, and renew a right spirit within me.

(Psalm 51:10)

A Prayer For You

Father God, I ask that each boy and girl ask your forgiveness for the wrongs that they have done to others, and that you give them the courage to ask those they have hurt to forgive them.

Chapter 8 Review

Asking Others to Forgive You

Define Forgiveness: to erase

1. Always be willing to say "I am sorry" to those you might have hurt.

2. Reasons it is sometimes hard for kids to say "I'm sorry" are:

   - Embarrassed

   - Sign of weakness

   - Promise themselves that they will never do the same wrong again

   - Thinking they will apologize later

   - Thinking that God will get mad at them

3. Memory Verse: Create in me a clean heart, O Lord, and renew a right spirit within me. (Psalm 51:10)

Chapter 8 Activities

Asking Others to Forgive You

Directions: To begin your activities for this chapter, Bubby will give you a scripture, an exercise, and a tip that will help boost your self-esteem. Next, will be questions for you to answer on the Bible story. Be sure to take time to memorize the memory verse and pray your own personal prayer. Finally, you will answer questions and do activities to check your understanding of *Asking Others to Forgive You*.

 Hi, kids! Do I ever have a scripture that tells something God did for you that you might not have even realized. Check it out in the box.

Self-Esteem means:

- How you feel about yourself
- The opinion you have of yourself
- How much value you place on yourself

God Created YOU With Special Gifts
"When He ascended up on high, He gave gifts (abilities) to His people." (Ephesians 4:8 KJV)

---

1. The scripture in the box says that God gave each person special gifts. That means that God you gave you an ability to do something that you are really good at doing.

   What are some of the things you are good at doing? Is it dancing? Drawing? Playing sports? That is the gift God has given you. List your gift or gifts on the blanks below.

   _____   _____

   _____   _____

   _____   _____

2. **Take a tip from me:** These gifts that you have are the things that God wants you to enjoy as well as use to help others in need. Start using them and your confidence will increase. Hop to it!

   Write out the sentence on the next page thanking God for the special gifts He has given you.

Thank you, God, for the special gifts you gave me. I want to use those gifts to help others.

_____

_____

3. Sometimes other people see gifts in us that we might not see. Ask the adult traveling with you to name gifts they see that God has given you.

_____

The Prodigal Son

4. In the blank provided, write down the memory verse from the Bible story about The Prodigal Son and then memorize it.

    - **Create in me a clean heart, O Lord, and renew a right spirit within me.** (Psalm 51:10)

    _____

    _____

5. Was the son in the story sorry he had hurt his father?   (Yes)   (No)

6. What did he do when he realized he was wrong?

    _____

    _____

7. Write a short prayer asking God to forgive you for the times you have hurt Him and others.

    _____

    _____

8. Now, let's see what other things you have learned about Asking Others to Forgive You. Start by writing out the definition of Forgiveness one more time.

   • **Forgiveness means to erase**

   _____

9. Kids sometimes use excuses or have reasons why it is hard for them to say "I'm sorry." Place a check mark beside the ones that applies to you.

   • Embarrassed
   • Sign of weakness
   • Promise themselves that they will never do the same wrong again
   • Thinking they will apologize later
   • Thinking that God will get mad at them

10. Now, let's think about the times you know you were rude and hurt someone. Wouldn't you like to ask them to forgive you? Sometimes, this is a little hard to do at first. If it is hard for you, use the three steps on the following pages to help make it easier for you.

Step 1: Draw a picture of a chair. In the blank space under the chair you have drawn, write the person's name to whom you have been rude.

Who is sitting in the chair?

_____

Who is sitting in the chair?

_____

Who is sitting in the chair?

_____

Who is sitting in the chair?

_____

Step 2: Since it may be a little hard at first to face the person you hurt, practice how you want to tell them you are sorry in one of the following ways.

A. Write out what you would say if you talked to them face-to-face. Then stand before the mirror and practice saying it.

B. Another way you might want to say "I'm sorry" is by making them a card and writing a note inside of it.

C. Be sure to do this for each person you named in Step 1. Use the space below and the next page for this exercise.

Step 3: Now, write a simple prayer asking God to give you courage to go to the person or persons and ask them to forgive you for the hurt you have caused them, using the way you chose in Step 2.

_____

_____

_____

 **Next Stop:** On this stop, you did a really big thing when you Asked Others to Forgive You. Now it is time to move on to the next stop: **Accepting Losses**. Remember: God Created YOU With Special Gifts!

The Prodigal Son- Coloring Page

He made a bad choice that hurt himself and his father. Luke 15: 11-24

The Prodigal Son - -Coloring Page

He asked his father to forgive him for his bad choices. Luke 15: 11-24

**Create in me a clean heart, O God,
and renew a right spirit within me.**

Psalm 51:10

Additional Questions, Notes, and Drawings

Helping Hurting Children: A Journey of Healing – Children's Workbook

Chapter 9

Accepting Losses

"You did it! You did it!" You made it to the last stop on your ***Journey of Healing***. You have come a long way, and I am so proud of you.

On this stop, let's take a look at what Accepting Losses means by starting with the definition of accept.

> ### Accept means to agree to (1)

What this definition means as it pertains to losses is this: When we agree to the fact that we have experienced a particular loss, we can then move forward and <u>continue to be happy</u>.

No doubt you are shouting: "No way! There is no way I will ever agree to the loss I experienced. What I lost was something very valuable and special to me. I can't agree to that! It should have never happened."

Sometimes to understand the meaning of a word, it helps to know <u>what it does not mean.</u> For example:

➤ To accept does not mean that you like the fact you experienced a particular loss. We have to accept a lot of things in life. But, we do not have to like the fact that we lost someone or something of special value to us.(2)

➤ When we don't accept the fact that we have had a particular loss, you might say that we are actually rejecting what happened. When we reject it, we will keep thinking about the effects the loss had on our life and be miserable and unhappy.

✾ ✾ ✾ ✾ ✾ ✾ ✾ ✾ ✾ ✾ ✾ ✾

Bubby wants to tell you a story about his physical heart; the heart that keeps him alive and breathing. Here's what Bubby said happened.

I had been having problems breathing a long time, and was very sick. The vet told me that he wanted to operate on me. During the operation, he would give me a new heart in place of the one that was sick. He also told me that sometimes a rabbit's body might reject the new heart for reasons that he didn't really understand. If the body rejected it, the rabbit would continue to be sick. But, the vet felt confident that my body would accept it. So, I took his advice, and checked into the hospital.

I lay down on the operating table. The vet took out my old sick heart, and gave me a brand new heart for the one that was sick. Guess what? It worked. My body accepted the new heart, and now I can breathe so much better with my new heart. I am now enjoying life once again.

✾ ✾ ✾ ✾ ✾ ✾ ✾ ✾ ✾ ✾ ✾ ✾

Now, let me talk this word "accept" out with you as it pertains to your wounded heart, that part of you that hurts when you experience a loss. Let's start at the beginning of your ***Journey of Healing.***

On one of the very first stops of your journey, you learned that all losses hurt inside. They hurt so much that it feels like a big bolt of lightning has hit you right in your heart. Remember this wounded heart is not your physical heart that makes you breathe. It's that deep part inside of you where your feelings and emotions live that cannot be seen.

The Lord saw your hurt; He was with you. Because He knew what it felt like to hurt inside, He sent His son, Jesus to forgive you of your sins and also to heal your broken-heart.

One of the first things Jesus did to start healing your broken heart was to send an adult friend into your life. This special person listened to you as you poured out your feelings about the loss you had experienced, and he comforted you as well.

Your adult friend also helped you learn how to forgive those people who hurt you. This friend then gave you an opportunity to ask others to forgive you for the wrong things you did to them.

The only thing left to do now is accept the "new heart" that Jesus is offering to you for the one that was wounded. It is with your new heart that you can continue to enjoy life, even in the midst of your loss. Make sure you understand that you do not have to like the fact that you have been separated from someone or something that had special value to you. You only have to agree it has happened, so you can continue to enjoy life.

Three ways you can know you have Accepted Your Loss:(3)

1. You know you have Accepted Your Loss when <u>you can talk</u> about the loss freely and it just <u>does not sting</u> you like it once did.

When you first experience a loss, it is so hard to talk about the person or thing that you lost. It feels like it is tearing your insides out. One of the first ways you can know you have accepted the loss is when you realize you can talk about your loss freely with other people and it just doesn't sting and feel like it is tearing you up inside like it once did.

2. You know you have Accepted Your Loss when you begin to have <u>good memories</u>.

Good memories come as a result of things you have <u>learned</u> that comforted you during the time of your loss. On this ***Journey of Healing***, someone has traveled with you listening, comforting, and guiding you while your heart was breaking. You learned many things from them, and you will always have good memories of what they did for you and what you learned during this time.

3. You know you have Accepted Your Loss when <u>you can help others</u> who are going through losses in their lives.

There is no greater joy in life than helping others. You will know that you have accepted your loss when you want to begin helping other boys and girls who might be experiencing losses in their lives.

❋ ❋ ❋ ❋ ❋ ❋ ❋ ❋ ❋ ❋ ❋

Let's see if our Journey Friends have arrived at Acceptance of their loss.

Helping Hurting Children: A Journey of Healing – Children's Workbook

Experiences of our Journey Friends

Hadley

1. I can talk freely to others about my dad's death and it doesn't sting me anymore.

I still think about my dad every day. But, now I think about the fun times we had and what a good daddy he was. I love hearing stories other people tell me about Daddy. They make me laugh.

2. Things I learned

I joined a Support Group for children who had experienced a death in their family, and I learned some very valuable lessons.

- I learned how to express my feelings about dad's death, and still have good behavior.

- I finally realized my dad's death was not my fault. There was nothing that I could have done to have prevented his death.

- I learned that I was not responsible for my mother's happiness.

- Nobody could take dad's place, but I learned other ways to be happy.

3. I can help others

One of the things that helped me the most was having someone listen to me when I expressed my feelings. That is how I want to help others.

Crystal

1. I can talk freely to others about Jay bullying me and it doesn't sting anymore.

My mom and I talked with the Guidance Counselor at my school, and also my children's church pastor. Talking helped me to get my feelings out, plus I was no longer carrying a secret around with me. It doesn't sting me to think and talk about it like it once did.

2. Things I Learned

When Mom and I talked to the Guidance Counselor at my school, I learned some valuable lessons about bullying.

- Do not fight back!
- Always tell an adult when you are being bullied. "Telling is not tattling."
- I learned to forgive Jay for all the bad things he had said and done to me.

3. I can help others

One of the ways that I want to help others who are being bullied is to go with them to tell an adult about what is happening to them. I will not be a bystander ever again.

Heather

1. **I can talk freely to others about moving to a new city and it doesn't sting me anymore.**

   Leaving all my friends behind in New Orleans no longer hurts me like it once did. I still write to them, call them on the phone, and visit. They will always have a special place in my heart.

2. **Things I learned**

   - I learned that I did not lose my friends in New Orleans when I moved.

   - I learned to forgive the two girls at my new school for being so rude to me.

   - The best thing I learned is that you can make new friends wherever you go.

3. **I can help others**

   Making a move to a new city helped me realize a very important lesson and that is: "I should always be a friend to the new kid in school."

Hannah

1. **I can talk freely to others about the death of my pet and it doesn't sting me anymore.**

   No other pet will ever replace Fala in my heart. I keep the memory of Fala with me always in a memory album I made of him. I take it out and read about all the fun times we had together. He makes me laugh.

2. **Things I learned**

   I learned that I have a lot of love to give. I want to give that love to another pet.

3. **I can help others**
   - Volunteering in an animal shelter
   - Comforting others who have lost a pet

Zach

1. I can talk freely to others about my parents' divorce and it doesn't sting me anymore.

My parents' divorce no longer hurts me like it once did. I wish it had never happened, but when I talk about it now, I talk about the fun times we had like vacation trips in our camper. The funniest memory I have is seeing Dad operate the camera on Christmas morning.

2. Things I learned

I joined a Support Group for children of divorce, and I learned a lot.

- It is okay for boys to cry.
- It is okay to tell my parents exactly what I'm feeling.
- The divorce was not my fault.
- I can't fix my parents' problems.
- I can do fun things with Dad, even though we live in separate houses.
- I forgave my parents for hurting me.
- I asked my parents and brother to forgive me for being rude to them.

3. I can help others

I want to comfort other kids whose parents divorce, and pass on to them all the lessons I learned during the time of my parents' divorce.

✻ ✻ ✻ ✻ ✻ ✻ ✻ ✻ ✻ ✻ ✻

Looks like all the kids traveling with us on our **_Journey of Healing_** came to the place that they accepted their loss. I am so excited for them that they have a new beginning in life in spite of their loss. And YOU can, too!

Boys, and girls, I will be honest with you and say that, even though you have learned so much at each of these stops on your journey, it may take a little while to get back to the "old you" before your loss. You see, healing a broken heart is just like healing a broken leg; it takes a little time to recover, but you can do it! Healing is a process.

But, the more you talk out your feelings, keep on forgiving those who hurt you, and even asking others to forgive you, your wounded heart just begins to heal. You can then continue to enjoy life.

Bubby says: You did it! You did it! I am flipping out; I am so excited for you. Now you can have a new beginning in life. Go for it! I'm rooting for you!

Bible Story

Joseph and His Brothers

Genesis 37 - 50

The best Bible story I can tell you about Accepting a Loss is to finish the story of Joseph with whom we began our ***Journey of Healing***. We left off in our story when starving people from all over the world began arriving in Egypt to buy food during the famine.

You remember that Pharaoh had appointed Joseph as the Governor in all of Egypt. God had told Joseph that the famine was coming, and Joseph and the Egyptians had stored up food in preparation for it. And now the famine has hit, and thousands of people are coming daily begging to buy food from the Egyptians under Joseph's leadership.

Suddenly, among the thousands of people standing face-to-face with Joseph were his brothers. Joseph immediately recognized them, but they did not recognize their little brother, who was now the governor of Egypt. All they had on their minds was buying food to take back home to their aging father.

Before we see what happened in that face-to-face encounter between Joseph and his brothers, let's review the losses Joseph experienced at the hands of his brothers.

Perhaps those losses are running through his mind now as he looks into the face of his brothers.

- His brothers hated him because they thought their father loved him more

- His brothers stole his coat of many different colors

- His brothers threw him into a deep pit

- His brothers sold him to traders going to a faraway country

- He was separated from his father

- He lost his boyhood home and the country in which he was born

Certainly, Joseph did not like the fact that all these losses occurred in his life. Can you just imagine what he must have been feeling the day his brothers sold him to traders going to a faraway country? He didn't know it then, but he was going to have to live many years away from his father.

However, Joseph knew that **God was with him**, and he responded with a good attitude and behavior to what was happening to him. The Bible also tells the story of Joseph's life away from his father all those years. It was during these years that he experienced even more losses.

But, Joseph kept on responding with a good attitude and behavior. Obviously, he had learned at an early age one or more of the OKAY WAYS you learned about in chapter 6 to pour out his feelings, complaints, and praises to God throughout the years. I know his father would have been so proud of him.

Now back to the face-to-face encounter between Joseph and his brothers. There they are, looking into the eyes of Joseph and had not even recognized him. Joseph could hardly contain himself. As a matter of fact, he left the meeting and went into a room and wept.

Finally, Joseph makes himself known to his brothers. "I am Joseph. Is my father still alive?" (Genesis 45:3 KJV) Fear gripped them, wondering what he was going to do to them. No doubt all the mean things they had done to Joseph flashed before them. They immediately bowed down to Joseph, giving him honor and asking him to forgive them of the wrong things they had done to him when he was a young boy.

Joseph could have had his brothers killed on the spot, but he said to them,

"You intended to harm me, but
God intended it all for good.

He brought me to this position
so I could save the lives of many people."

(Genesis 50:20 NLT)

What Can You Learn From the Life of Joseph?

Not only did Joseph forgive his brothers, but he helped his brothers when they were experiencing a loss. He also helped thousands of other people who were experiencing a loss.

When we experience a loss, and we allow God to help us with our feelings about that loss, as well as forgive others who have hurt us, we can then accept the loss and help others going through a loss also.

It is then that we have a new beginning in life, and our joy returns, despite the loss. That is what *Grieving a Loss* is all about.

Memory Verse

You intended to harm me, but God intended it all for good. He brought me to this position so I could save the lives of many people.

(Genesis 50:20)

A Prayer For You

Father God, I pray for each boy and girl who has experienced losses in their life. I pray that they have reached a place of accepting their loss and can now move forward to a new beginning in life, and that they will continue to enjoy their life.

Chapter 9 Review

Accepting Losses

Define Accept: To agree to

1. To accept does not mean you like losing; it means you don't reject it in order to move on and continue to enjoy life.

2. Three ways you can know you have accepted a loss are:

   (1) When you can talk about the loss freely and it does not sting you like it once did.

   (2) When you begin to have good memories of what you learned during the time of your loss.

   (3) When you can help others who are going through losses in their lives.

3. Memory Verse: You intended to harm me, but God intended it all for good. He brought me to this position so I could save the lives of many people. (Genesis 50:20)

Chapter 9 Activities

Accepting Losses

Directions: To begin your activities for this chapter, Bubby will give you a scripture, an exercise, and a tip that will help boost your self-esteem. Next, will be questions for you to answer on the Bible story. Be sure to take time to memorize the memory verse and pray your own personal prayer. Finally, you will answer questions and do activities to check your understanding of *Accepting Losses*.

 Hi, kids! My last self-esteem scripture for you will make you jump sky high with joy as you learn more about it. Get ready!

Self-esteem means:

- How you feel about yourself
- The opinion you have of yourself
- How much value you place on yourself

God Comforts YOU
YOU Can Comfort Others
He comforts us in all our troubles so that we can comfort others. When they are troubled, we will be able to give them the same comfort God has given us. (II Corinthians. 1:4 NLT)

1. Think about the ***Journey of Healing*** you have been traveling. Do you feel you were comforted for the loss you experienced? If so, how?

   _____

   _____

2. What does the scripture in the box tells you to do about the comfort you have received from God?

   _____

3. **Take a tip from me:** Helping others brings you a whole lot of joy. In fact, it will make you feel good about yourself because you have comforted someone in need. So, always be on the look-out for ways to comfort and help others.

   Write out the sentence on the next page thanking God for comforting you.

• Thank you, God, for comforting me. Help me to comfort others.

_____

_____

Joseph and His Brothers

4. In the blank provided, write down the memory verse from the Bible story about Joseph and His Brothers, and then memorize it.

  • **You intended to harm me, but God intended it for good. He brought me to this position to save the lives of many people.** (Genesis 50:20)

_____

_____

5. Think about Joseph's life starting from the time his father asked him to bring his brothers food to the field where they were working. Answer each question in the blanks.

  (1) Who does the Bible say was with Joseph when he experienced his losses?

  _____

  (2) How would you describe Joseph's attitude when he came face to face with his brothers when they came to Egypt to buy food? Circle your answer.

          Rude and Mean   Frightened   Christ-like

  (3) Would you say that Joseph forgave his brothers, even though they had done him so wrong? (Yes) (No)

  (4) Did Joseph help his brothers in time of their need? (Yes) (No)

  (5) Would you say that Joseph accepted his losses, and continued to enjoy life, in spite of his losses? (Yes) (No)

6. Write a short prayer asking God to help you to always be willing to help others in times of their need.

_____

_____

 **Accepting Losses**

7. Now, let's see what you learned about Accepting Losses. You can start by writing the definition of accept on the lines provided.

   • **Accept means to agree to**

_____

8. When you agree to accepting a particular loss in your life, does that mean you have to like the fact you lost someone or something of value to you?
   (Yes)   (No)

9. Does agreeing to accept your loss mean that you can continue to enjoy life?
   (Yes)   (No)

10. On the following pages are listed the three ways in which you know you have accepted your loss. Answer each of these ways in your own words.

I can talk about the loss freely and it just doesn't STING me like it once did.

_____

_____

_____

_____

Important things I learned from this experience are:

_____

_____

_____

I can help others who are experiencing a loss by:

_____

_____

_____

Joseph and His Brothers – Coloring Page

"You intended to harm me, but
God intended it all for good.

He brought me to this position
so I could save the lives of many people."

Genesis 50:20

Additional Questions, Notes, and Drawings

Last Stop: What a journey you have had! You have only one more stop to make and I can't wait for you to get there. Remember: YOU Can Comfort Others.

Chapter 10

Last Stop on the Journey

Hi, kids! It's me, Bubby, with a BIG announcement.

The Winner of Bubby's Self-Esteem Blue Ribbon is ---

<u>YOU</u>!

I popped in along your journey and gave you Bible verses and tips on **Self-Esteem**. I believe that you now feel good about yourself, have a high opinion of yourself, and place high value on yourself because you learned through this journey how God sees you. And that is what self-esteem is all about.

Having a high self-esteem is not bragging about yourself. Self-esteem gives you confidence that will enable you to become the person that God has created you to be. With that confidence, you will always be a winner, even when you experience losses in your life.

Let's check in with the kids who traveled on this journey with us to see what they learned about self-esteem.

Experiences of our Journey Friends

Hadley

The self-esteem tip that helped me the most was learning just **how valuable I am to God.** I always felt that my feelings and opinions did not count to my friends and family. So, I started keeping all my thoughts and feelings closed up inside of me, afraid to voice them.

When I learned that Jesus always had time for children, and that my feelings and opinions were important to Him, it changed how I felt about myself. It gave me confidence in myself, as well as feeling so valued.

I would like to become a writer with the gifts God gave me.

Crystal

The self-esteem tip that helped me to regain my self-esteem was learning all the **names that God calls me.** I replaced all those rude names Jay called me like stupid, ugly, and cry-baby with the names that God calls me.

I couldn't believe that the creator of the universe calls me names like BOLD, CONQUEROR, FRIEND. It made me have confidence in myself.

I just know that one day my dream will come true of owning my own health fitness business.

Heather

Before I moved from my home in New Orleans, I was sort of popular with the other kids in my neighborhood, school, and church. But, when I made the move, I felt like I was a "nobody." I began losing confidence in myself.

But, when I learned that God had **placed gifts within me**, it changed everything. I began to realize that the gifts God had given me were not left in my old city, they moved with me. God gave them to me for my enjoyment and to help others no matter where I live.

My dream is to be a writer and a dance chorographer when I grow up using the gifts God gave me when He created me.

Hannah

I became so shy after my pet dog, Fala, died. I guess it was because I stayed in my room so much crying after his death. I stayed there so long that I forgot how to play with other kids. Finally, I learned that God's love for me is higher than the heavens. It gave me the confidence to walk outside into the world again and all my shyness began to leave.

I have a dream to become a professional soccer player when I grow up, or a creative writer. I know I can do it.

Zach

When my parents got a divorce, I made a lot of bad choices, like fighting, yelling, and just being rude to everyone. Sometimes I knew that I was acting bad, but I didn't care anymore how I looked or sounded to anybody. I actually began to dislike my own self because of the choices I was making.

But, when I learned that God gives me courage to make right choices, I began to take responsibility for my actions. I can't believe that just choosing to make good choices helped me have confidence and feel good about myself.

My dream is to be a fireman when I grow up. No, wait, I think I want to be a policeman. No, I want to be a Super Hero! Oh, I really don't know what I want to be yet. But, I know one thing for sure. I can be all that God created me to be!

❊ ❊ ❊ ❊ ❊ ❊ ❊ ❊ ❊ ❊ ❊

Just like you, the kids on our journey with us are winners. They learned just how valuable, loved, and special they are to God.

Your last Bible Story on your ***Journey of Healing*** tells about a young man named Jeremiah, who didn't value himself very much -- that is, until he learned just how much God valued him. Let's read it now.

Bible Story
The Call of Jeremiah
Jeremiah 1:4-8

The Bible tells the story of a young man whose name was Jeremiah. One day God spoke to Jeremiah and said, "I knew you before you were formed within your mother's womb; before you were born I sanctified you and appointed you as my spokesman to the world."   (Jeremiah 1:4-5 LB)

Jeremiah was only seventeen years old at the time God spoke these words to him. Wow! What a big job God wanted this teenager to do -- a spokesman to the whole world! That's awesome, isn't it?

However, Jeremiah didn't think it was so awesome. In fact, he didn't want to do it at all, so he said to God, "I can't do that! I cannot speak! I'm far too young! I'm only a youth!" (Jeremiah 1:6 LB)

Unfortunately, Jeremiah didn't think he had the ability to do what God had asked him to do. Obviously, he didn't place much value in himself, or have a high opinion of himself. In short, Jeremiah had not seen himself as God was seeing him.

But, God responded to Jeremiah by saying, "Don't say that, for you will go wherever I send you and speak whatever I tell you to. And don't be afraid of the people, for I, the Lord, will be with you and see you through." (Jeremiah 1:7-8 LB)

What was God saying to Jeremiah? I believe he was saying: "Jeremiah, you have value, worth, and special abilities I have given to you. You can do this! You can be my spokesman!" And that is exactly what Jeremiah went on to do.

"Just like Jeremiah, <u>YOU</u> can be all that God created you to be!"

Your Bunny Friend,

Bubby

How God Sees YOU

The Call of Jeremiah – Coloring Page

You will go wherever I send you and speak whatever I tell you to.
And don't be afraid of the people, for I, the Lord,
will be with you and see you through.

Jeremiah 1:7-8

Additional Questions, Notes, and Drawings

Notes

Chapter 1: Beginning the Journey

1. www.kidshealth.com

Chapter 2: What Does *"Loss"* Mean?

1. Wright, H. Norman, (2004). It's Okay to Cry. Water Brook Press. pg. 12.

Chapter 3: Facts About Losses

1. Wright, H. Norman, (2004). It's Okay to Cry. Water Brook Press. pg. 9.
2. Heegaard, Marge, (1988). When Someone Very Special Dies. Woodland Press. pg. 14.

Chapter 6: Expressing Feelings

1. Guralnik, David B., Editor in Chief, (1982), Webster's New World Dictionary. Simon and Schuster, pg. 355.
2. Moore, Beth, (1996). A Heart Like His. Life Way Press. pg. 52-53.

Chapter 8: Asking Others to Forgive You

1. Stanley, Charles, (1987). The Gift of Forgiveness. Thomas Nelson Publishers. pg. 195-196.

Chapter 9: Accepting Loss

1. Guralnik, David B., Editor in Chief, (1982), Webster's New World Dictionary. Simon and Schuster, pg. 3.
2. Teachings of the late Melba Berkeheimer, former co-pastor of Community Church, Orange, Texas.
3. Ibid.

Bible Translations

Verses marked NIV are taken from the New International Version.
Verses marked LB are taken from The Living Bible.
Verses marked NLT are taken from The New Living Bible.
Verses marked KJV are taken from King James Version.
Verses marked MSG are taken from The Message.
Verses marked HCSB are taken from Holman Christian Standard Bible.

Helping Hurting Children: A Journey of Healing – Children's Workbook

About the Author

Martha Bush grew up on a farm in Donalsonville, Georgia. She graduated from Valdosta State College, Valdosta, Georgia, with a BS degree in Business Education. After graduating from college, Martha began her teaching career that spanned grades 5-12 in both public and Christian schools. She also taught adult vocational courses in the Atlanta school system.

Her love for teaching led her into areas outside the school system as she began teaching Bible study courses in jails, prisons, and at her local church. She also writes a monthly inspirational post at www.createdwoman.net and is a contributing editor for *Created Woman Magazine*.

In addition, she is a contributor at www.girlfriendscoffeehour.com and a member of The Orange County Christian Writers Guild.

Through her years of teaching, as well as being an avid reader of human behavior and grief counseling from noted Christian psychologists, she recognized how a team effort can help build a foundation in children at an early age that will enable them to cope with the losses in their lives. She believes this team, made of up parents, grandparents, educators, and spiritual leaders, can guide a child to healing from losses he or she might experience. They can do this simply by recognizing his pain, listening to his pain, and then teaching the child how to apply the principles of God's Word to his hurting heart. This led her to write ***Helping Hurting Children: A Journey of Healing.***

Martha resides in Orange, Texas, with her husband, Glen. They are the parents of two grown daughters who have blessed them with three beautiful grandchildren.

Should you be interested in becoming a caring adult, visit www.marthafbush.com for more information on how you can purchase the books or email her at: martha@marthafbush.com.